Praise for *The Great Eight*

"For the past twenty-seven years, Scott Hamilton has been a mentor and good friend. I've seen firsthand the struggles he has had to endure and how he has continued to persevere with a confident attitude. He lives his life as a champion. Everyone needs the positive message of this greatly inspiring book."

—Kristi Yamaguchi
Olympic Gold Medalist

"I know and love Scotty Hamilton. You will, too, after you read this book."
—William Shatner

"Scott Hamilton is a champion in more ways than one. In addition to being one of the world's greatest ice skaters, he has mastered adversity and a multitude of challenges. *The Great Eight* is an inspiration to us all."
—Donald J. Trump

"Scott's outlook on life continues to influence me in a very positive way, encouraging me to look at challenges in a larger context. Within the metaphors of his skating career, the wisdom in this book is not only very inspiring and easy to grasp but also surrounded by great storytelling. I'm so glad he recorded it for the rest of us."

—Brad Paisley
Grammy Award-winning artist

"It's like my bud Scott says: 'You can't just skate through life and expect to be happy!' So anyone choosing not to buy this book is choosing *not* to be happy. Shame on you."

—Kevin Nealon
Actor, comedian, *Saturday Night Live* alum

"In each successive chapter and challenge in his remarkable life, Scott Hamilton has forged ahead with unquenchable spirit and uncommon joy, always emerging wiser than before. This warm and insightful book will allow its readers to experience the blessing I've been privileged to enjoy in person: a delightful, practical, bracingly honest conversation with one of our national treasures.

—Ken Durham, PhD
Senior Minister, The University Church of Christ
at Pepperdine University

"A gold medal literary performance from a true Olympic star."

—Richard D. Lamm
Governor of Colorado

"*The Great Eight* intertwines penetrating honesty with lighthearted practical insight, drawing common-sense analogies from the sport Scott loves—and that saved his life. This primer for building the thrill of victory and immortal gladness is written for everyone, regardless of age."

—Janet Lynn
Five-time US Champion, Ladies Figure Skating
Olympic Bronze Medalist, 1972

"Through a lifetime of facing incredible odds, Scott Hamilton has learned the secrets to maintaining a positive attitude and can-do spirit. Spend time in the pages of this book, and you will walk away truly inspired."

—Bob Kain
Former CEO, IMG
Current vice chairman, Cleveland Browns

"After a myriad of setbacks, Scott speaks eloquently about survival in the face of adversity. This book deserves a 'ten' and a 'Personal Best' too! Bravo!"

—Dick Button
Two-time Olympic Gold Medalist
Emmy Award-winning skating analyst

THE
GREAT EIGHT

THE
GREAT
EIGHT

How to Be Happy
(even when you have every reason to be miserable)

SCOTT HAMILTON
with KEN BAKER

THOMAS NELSON
Since 1798

NASHVILLE   DALLAS   MEXICO CITY   RIO DE JANEIRO   BEIJING

Published in Nashville, Tennessee, by Thomas Nelson. Thomas Nelson is a registered trademark of Thomas Nelson, Inc.

Thomas Nelson, Inc. titles may be purchased in bulk for educational, business, fund-raising, or sales promotional use. For information, please e-mail SpecialMarkets@ThomasNelson.com.

Optimist's Introduction: Scott Hamilton, *Landing It*: *My Life On and Off the Ice* (New York: Kensington Books, 1999). Used with permission.

Scripture quotations marked NIV are taken from Holy Bible: New International Version®. © 1973, 1978, 1984 by International Bible Society. Used by permission of Zondervan Publishing House. All rights reserved.

Scripture quotations marked ESV are taken from The English Standard Version. © 2001 by Crossway Bibles, a division of Good News Publishers.

Library of Congress Cataloging-in-Publication Data

Hamilton, Scott, 1958–
  The great eight : how to be happy (even when you have every reason to be miserable) /
Scott Hamilton.
     p. cm.
  Includes bibliographical references.
  ISBN 978-0-7852-2894-3 (hardcover)
  1. Happiness. I. Title.
  BF575.H27H36 2009
  158—dc22   2008035945

Printed in the United States of America

09 10 11 12 13 QW 9 8 7 6 5 4 3 2

This book is dedicated to my wife, Tracie,
who has taught me so much and given me more than
I could ever express in words.
I love you.

And also to Helen McLoraine.
Without you, I wouldn't be me.

CONTENTS

An Optimist's Introduction

Not long ago, I was giving a speech at a pituitary brain tumor conference at a hotel in Palm Springs. It was an intimate dinner gathering, with no more than fifty patients in the ballroom, and I was the keynote speaker.

I hadn't prepared a formal speech for the event. Instead, I wanted to give a casual, heartfelt speech about my experience of being diagnosed with a brain tumor in 2004, which led to me losing all function of my pituitary gland. I wanted the patients to learn how I, like many of them, was coping with the problems that come with not having a pituitary gland producing testosterone, adrenaline, steroids, and other biochemicals your body needs to survive. I shared a few details of my post-tumor daily routine: self-given injections in the thigh three times a week, testosterone gels, pills, and the emotional highs and lows that come with constantly fluctuating hormone levels. I discussed that due to the loss of physical strength and stamina, I had not skated in any serious way since the brain tumor, which—for an Olympic Gold Medalist, World Champion, and longtime professional figure skater—was the biggest bummer of all.

I talked about how the diagnosis and radiation treatment to kill the tumor (which unfortunately also destroyed my pea-size pituitary gland) came seven years after my bout with testicular cancer, a battle that cost me one of my testicles and brought my body to the brink.

I also shared about the blessings and joys in my life: In 2002, I married the love of my life, Tracie; and despite my hormonal problems, Tracie and I soon welcomed a son, Aidan, into our family. I expressed how my illnesses had brought me closer to God and made me appreciate life more than ever. I told this group of similarly suffering cancer patients that despite enduring all the pain, despite having to inject synthetic hormones into my thigh just to be healthy, and despite knowing that my glory years of professional skating were long behind me, I was still a pretty happy guy.

I have to admit, the look on their faces was one of surprise. There I was—vertically challenged, follically challenged, a survivor of testicular cancer and a brain tumor, an arguably washed-up former pro figure skater pushing fifty—claiming that I was happier than I had ever been in my entire life. Winning the Olympic Gold Medal in 1984? Performing in front of thousands every night for Stars on Ice? Hobnobbing with celebrities in Hollywood? Those things never made me happier than I was at that moment, standing before them, telling my survivor's story. As hard as it might have been for them to believe, it was the truth.

> "Scott, you have every reason to be miserable, but you're the happiest guy I've ever met. What's your secret?"

Afterward, a fellow brain tumor survivor came up to me and said, "Scott, you have every reason to be miserable, but you're the happiest guy I've ever met. What's your secret?"

His question sort of threw me. I had never thought about having some kind of "secret" to finding happiness. Like I had said in the speech, I felt that I had been blessed in many ways, yet I didn't really think I had any secret outlook on life. I just always considered myself an optimist.

The more I considered it, the more I realized that I did have a certain perspective on things that allowed me to be happy no matter what was thrown my way. And the more I looked around, the more I began noticing that other people might benefit from learning about how I am able to be happy after all I have been through. Like so many coaches had done for me over the years, I wanted to give everyone a pep talk and some helpful advice. That's why I wrote this book.

Initially, it was hard to translate my lifelong philosophy into a practical guide for others to find optimism and joy. I am not very good at telling people what to do, and I certainly have never tried to pass myself off as some sort of guru—even about figure skating. But I do like to tell stories. So in this book, you will read a lot of stories about experiences that taught me invaluable lessons about how to be happy. And the more I reflected on these life lessons, the more I realized how much skating had taught me about overcoming challenges in my life away from the ice.

Learning to Make a Great Figure Eight

Skating itself posed an enormous challenge to me from the very beginning. As a little kid learning to figure skate, there was one thing I hated doing more than anything: figure eights. Yet for several hours a day, my instructors required me to precisely (and tediously) carve the shape of an eight into the ice while balancing on one blade edge at a time. Using the outside edge of my right skate blade for one circle, then changing quickly to the left skate's outside edge for the second circle, I would attempt to trace over the lines perfectly again and again. The circles were more than twice my height in diameter and had to be created on a clean sheet of ice without any visible guides to help me. Just as I would later learn about creating a happy life, in order to make a great figure eight, I

> I had to face challenges and setbacks and, at times, I would doubt my abilities, but in order to succeed, I had to find my own way.

had to face challenges and setbacks and, at times, I would doubt my abilities, but in order to succeed, I had to find my own way.

For a goofy nine-year-old kid, it was hard enough to walk in a straight line, let alone skate in a circle while gliding on slippery ice! I would sometimes get lucky and manage to balance well enough to draw accurate tracings. But most of the time I would zigzag or fall down or simply grow bored and hurry through the exercise because I wanted to get to the fun stuff: skating fast, doing leaps and spins like an Olympic champion, and learning the acrobatic moves that make figure skating so enjoyable.

But my instructors would have none of it. They explained that if I didn't develop the fundamental skills that come only from repetitively practicing figure eights, I would never be able to execute the fun, flashy, sophisticated moves and become a world-class skater. Though doing so under major, bratty protest, I agreed to try harder at my figure eights.

The first thing I realized was that it was tedious work, and I really didn't have the patience for it. I mean, tracing lines repeatedly was plain boring. I've always been the kind of person who would have more energy running twenty miles in a straight course than doing five miles around track. At least with a course, I would constantly have some fresh scenery. As if the repeated circle making wasn't enough to bore me, I couldn't make any noise and couldn't play music. In other words, no distractions were allowed, which turned out to be the best thing about practicing figure eights because it forced me to develop focus and patience.

The coach would draw two circles on the ice, eight feet in

diameter and side-by-side so they connected to form an eight. Then I would have to trace over the line on one foot at a time, balancing on my blade's edges. The better I was able to trace over the line, the higher my score.

You start out just going around two small circles, and then soon you're doing three circles. Then you're making tiny circles within tiny circles, and then you're going forward and backward, and you're rotating against your body. You're having to do all this on perfect circles without any wobbles or any wiggles, and to do this you have to push off in the same place every time while also being mindful of your speed. Go too fast, and you can easily get off track; go too slow, and you lose balance. The deeper I got into the art of tracing figures, the more the challenge appealed to me. What had at first seemed boring now presented itself as a complex, fascinating challenge to my body. All the details matter: shoulder position, hip positioning, weight distribution on your edges, the direction of your gaze, your breathing. In other words, everything mattered.

As I practiced every day with repetition and consistency, I was building all the small muscles that gave me the ability to control my movements. I was mastering the fundamentals.

In each session, I would draw onto the ice two interconnecting circles and then make several attempts to trace over the markings as closely as I could. Before I knew it, I came to enjoy the repetition and practice and the challenge of making the tracings as perfectly on top of each other as possible, manipulating my inside and outside blade edges in pursuit of making a perfect figure eight. As I got better at making the figures and the lines became closer in shape and precision, my overall skating improved. True to what my coaches told me, the kids who had trouble doing figures struggled with basic skills when performing the fun, athletic stuff. They grew unhappy, and many eventually quit the sport altogether out of frustration.

Practicing my figures became such a major part of my training regime that in the months leading up to my 1984 Olympic Gold Medal victory, I would start each day spending three to four hours working on the repetition of these basic compulsory shapes; then, after rehearsing my short program, I would spend at least another hour practicing the figures.

> Like carving a perfect figure eight, finding happiness didn't come to me without enduring unhappy times.

As I will describe in more detail in chapter 4, the main reason I won the Gold Medal at the 1984 Olympics was because I was the best at figures. I turned the challenge of doing figures into a personal competition. I wanted to see how well I could do them. By the time I reached the 1984 season, I had them down better than anyone else. I knew that I was as good as anyone in the world, and if I won the figures at the Olympics, it would be next to impossible for me to lose the Gold Medal.

That so-called kid stuff paid off for me in a major way. In the wake of my Olympic victory, I was regarded as the world's most prolific male figure skater and since that time have been blessed to enjoy career successes beyond my wildest dreams. Most important, I have lived a good life. Although I can credit my happiness and success to many factors, everything I've learned about how to find happiness stems from what I learned through the repetition and discipline of perfecting my figure eights. And it's those vital life lessons that form the heart of the inspiring message I will share in this book.

But like carving a perfect figure eight, finding happiness didn't come to me without enduring unhappy times.

Living to Win Again

Perhaps my lowest point came in November 2004. At that time, I had assumed my greatest life problems were behind me. Seven years earlier, I had been diagnosed with testicular cancer. Painful surgery and chemotherapy—not to mention a lot of tears and prayer—got me through it alive. I beat that cancer into remission, and I had a whole new lease on life.

I assumed I had knocked aside my biological opponent, just as I had so many competitors on the ice during my skating career. I mean, everyone knows that lightning never strikes the same place twice, right?

> I believe that if you put my eight secrets to happiness into action, you will be able to find lasting happiness.

Then, with the odds presumably stacked in my favor that I would be enjoying an illness-free future, I wrote a memoir in 1999 sharing my comeback tale. Soon, I returned to my fast-paced life of ice shows, television broadcasting, public speaking, movie acting, golfing, and all the things that at the time I *thought* comprised my recipe for winning the game of life.

Then came the bad news—again. It was yet another medical crisis that I wouldn't wish upon my worst enemy: a brain tumor. Besides reminding me that I am not invincible and am only here by the grace of God, this medical malady would teach me that I had abandoned many of the practices that over my life had won me friends, love, fame, wealth, and business success. Facing death yet again, I realized I was no longer living to win. Rather, I was living to not lose. The difference between the two marks the difference between the runner-up and the champion, the demoted and the promoted, the unhappy and the happy. When I started to realize this simple yet profound fact, I began to rediscover what I had forgotten: the secrets behind my lifelong success, fulfillment, and happiness.

THE GREAT EIGHT

So why are there *eight* secrets to finding happiness? First of all, the number eight has been special for me going back to being born on August 28, 1958 (08-28-58). Plus, I've always considered eight my lucky number and consistently shun lists of the usual ten in favor of those of eight.

Eight is also a lucky number in China. While in Bejing for the 2008 Summer Olympics, I could not help but notice the significance the Chinese place on the number eight, which they associate with prosperity and confidence. The games' opening ceremonies were even scheduled for 08-08-08.

At the core of a figure skater's training regime, the number eight played a profound role throughout my skating life. Skaters perfect their skills through intense practice of carving a figure eight in the ice without error while balancing on one skate! If you cut the number eight in half—vertically or horizontally—the halves mirror themselves. Perfect symmetry lends itself to perfect balance. And in the Chinese culture, perfect balance is considered the ideal. And so it is also on the ice.

If executed with accuracy, the exact placement of each line should leave no evidence of a beginning or end. It takes years of dedication and practice for a skater to create a perfect figure eight, and it's no different in one's pursuit of happiness.

Perhaps the greatest significance of the number eight is that when you lay it on its side, it is the symbol for infinity. Fittingly, I believe that if you put my eight secrets to happiness into action, you will be able to find *lasting* happiness.

Without practicing the fundamental skills of anything—be it skating, golf, tennis, teaching, sales, marketing, writing, or mowing lawns—you can't reach your potential. One of the most tragic examples of what can go wrong when one strays from the discipline and practice of fundamental skills can be found in the world of modern figure skating. From the beginning of competitive figure skating, skaters were required in every competition to perform what were called the *compulsory figures*—essentially, the carving of eights and other figures into the ice, as previously described. A skater's total score was a combination of the compulsory figures and his performance routine. Then in 1990, the International Skating Union eliminated compulsory figures from competition because the powers-that-be didn't think they mattered anymore and, even more unfortunate, that television audiences weren't interested in seeing skaters balancing slowly on edges over small patches of ice.

Then what happened? Predictably, young skaters soon stopped practicing their figures. Instead, their coaches had them focus on jumps and spins and all the TV-friendly moves that give figure skating high ratings. With even the most elite skaters no longer practicing the precision and balance exercises, the quality of skating in the sport has suffered greatly. Skaters now lack the muscle strength that figures give, so injuries have increased. Further, many skaters have lost their overall mastery of the fundamental skills that performing compulsory figures had developed: agility, balance, posture, stamina, and concentration. To state it simply, modern skaters are incredible athletes, but because many of them have not mastered agility, balance, posture, stamina, and concentration, they are not as good at skating as their predecessors.

The same can be said for why so many people today find themselves unhappy: they have stopped practicing the basic principles of happiness. All of us must learn these fundamentals, one at a time, and repeat them to the point where we eventually can build up our *happiness* muscle strength in order to master the skills outlined in this book and execute them well without even thinking about it.

The Great Eight outlines my fundamental secrets to being happy. I hope they also will become yours.

CHAPTER ONE

Fall, Get Up, and Land Your First Jumps

The first time I ever skated, I fell flat on my back. As a matter of fact, the same could be said for the start of just about everything I have tried to do in my life: I fall down.

Whether learning to skate, to love, to succeed in business, or more recently, to play the drums, I have a good track record of making a total fool out of myself. But I've never let a losing start discourage me from trying to have a winning finish. It just takes committing to the task and being willing to fall down—a lot.

Of all the things I have tried in my life, skating is the best example of the happiness I have found after sticking to something, even when the beginning was a profound disaster.

I

Anyone who claims to have been a "born skater" is either lying or a one-in-a-million exception who, frankly, I have yet to meet. And I've met a lot of skaters! The simple truth is that the first time we step on the ice, we all end up on our backsides, not to mention in some level of pain.

A SLIPPERY START

My introduction to skating came on a frozen driveway across the street from my childhood home in Bowling Green, Ohio. I was four years old, and it was the dead of winter in northern Ohio. There's not much for a kid to do in that part of the country during the winter. The frozen driveways in our neighborhood provided the only semblance of a playground for kids.

> Of all the things I have tried in my life, skating is the best example of the happiness I have found after sticking to something, even when the beginning was a profound disaster.

My neighbors across the street had the smoothest sheet of ice on their driveway. My parents, wanting me to get out of the house for a little while, bundled me up in a warm jacket, mittens, a wool hat, and a tiny pair of skates with double runners—the skating equivalent of training wheels. My parents figured I would have fun and, since the blades (two on each skate) were so wide, even a fragile and sickly child like me couldn't do much harm to himself.

2

Well, they were wrong. After watching other kids cruise around the driveway with ease, I figured, *Hey, I can do that!* So my parents stood me up on the ice, let go of me, and I eagerly set off for my first skating experience. After a few moments of tentative skating, I fell backward!

My skates went out from under me, whipping my body back violently. I toppled backward, crashed onto my upper back, and then the back of my head landed—*smack!*—onto the concrete-hard ice like a dropped bowling ball.

I burst into tears, absolutely howling. I just wanted my mommy to take me home. I cried and cried and cried. Forty-five years later, I can still remember being that little kid and bawling my eyes out. Safe to say, I never wanted to get back on the ice. And according to my parents, I vowed to never, ever put those stupid skates on my feet again!

A violent spill like that would be traumatic enough for any kid, but the inglorious launch of my skating career was especially scary because, up until that time in my life, I had already experienced a lifetime's worth of physical and emotional trauma. In fact, I had been falling down in life for as long as I could remember.

FIGHTING FOR LIFE

As a child, I suffered through what can only be described as a mystery illness that prevented me from digesting my food normally and, ultimately, kept me from growing. My doctors in Bowling Green couldn't figure out what was wrong with me. No matter what remedies they offered, I only got worse. I wasn't eating, wasn't grow-ing, and my strength was weakening every day. Because I was adopted and had no medical history provided by my birth parents, the doctors didn't have any genetic clues to my mystery malady.

Most of my childhood memories are a blur of undergoing medi-cal tests, spending nights in hospitals, swallowing foul-tasting medicines, and being driven to hospitals all over the country by my mom in search of a cure for my illness. When the doctors in Bowling Green couldn't help me, my mom took me to the medical center in nearby Toledo. When they didn't know what to make of me, I was taken to the children's hospital at the University of Michigan in Ann Arbor, where my parents were told the best doc-tors certainly would be able to cure me. After spending several days giving me tests, exams, feeding me through a tube, you name it, the physicians and medical staff there came to a conclusion: they had no clue what was causing my problems. The best they could find was that I was suffering from malabsorption syndrome, mean-ing that rather than digesting my food, my body would reject it and get rid of it as fast as possible.

I was almost nine by then, and I had not grown since I was about four and a half years old. I was half the height of my peers and was very underdeveloped muscularly. Pale and weak, I also had a distended stomach because I was malnourished from not being able to absorb nutrients into my body.

Most embarrassing of all, I had a feeding tube in my nose. My parents had to feed me a liquid mixture of vitamins, but because it tasted so chalky, the only way to get me to take it was through a feeding tube. The supplements tasted so gross that I would go to the toilet and gag after eating them. Sometimes I would run to the bathroom and secretly spit them out in the sink so I wouldn't have to put that horrible-tasting stuff in my body. So the only way my parents could make sure that these vitamins and supplements went into my body was to hook up a bottle of this junk to a tube that went up my nose, down my esophagus, and directly into my stomach. That was how they fed it to me. As you can imagine, it was not a pleasant experience, though I realized that the tube was enabling me to stay alive.

> One of the many characteristics I learned from my parents was a never-take-no-for-an-answer attitude.

A few of the dozens of doctors my parents consulted suggested I suffered from extreme food allergies (I had to run to the bathroom minutes after eating almost anything), so my parents put me on a very restricted diet of no wheat, no flour, no sugar, no dairy. Yet my condition was only getting worse. My parents feared they were running out of time.

The top doctor at Ann Arbor's University Hospital concluded, "If things don't change soon, I don't think he will survive much longer." Now that I have two precious children of my own, I can't imagine how horrible it was for my parents to hear that grim diagnosis.

However, one of the many characteristics I learned from my parents was a never-take-no-for-an-answer attitude. Lucky for me, they decided they'd had enough of hospitals with no answers. Rather than accept my morbid fate, they were determined to reverse it.

That's when we went to Children's Hospital Boston, where a well-respected doctor named Harry Shwachman had done a lot of research on children who had trouble digesting food and experienced stunted growth. He had even named the illness Shwachman-Diamond syndrome. Of course, no parent wants his or her child to be diagnosed with any disease, but in my case, my mom and dad were hoping that Dr. Shwachman *would* diagnose me so that, perhaps, I could start getting proper treatment.

In Boston, Dr. Shwachman put me through every test you could imagine. He concluded that I didn't have Shwachman-Diamond syndrome, I didn't have cystic fibrosis (which I had previously been diagnosed with by another doctor), and I also didn't have any of the myriad of diseases that various doctors suspected I was suffering from.

> If I had even the slightest chance at overcoming my illness, at saving my life, it was a fight I would have to win by myself, for myself.

He told my parents, "I can't find what's causing this, so let's just go under the assumption that we're overtreating and panicking." The doctor's counterintuitive approach made sense to my parents, who had grown frustrated by getting nothing out of trying everything in the book!

Dr. Shwachman suggested, "Go home. Take him off the restricted diet. Help him live a normal life, and see what happens. We have nothing to lose."

By that point, my parents were exhausted from all the traveling, medical care, sleeping in hospitals, restricted diets, and everything else. Now that I am a parent, I cannot imagine the fear, anxiety, helplessness, and heartbreak my parents endured watching me suffer every day.

Back home in Bowling Green, my parents tried to follow Dr. Shwachman's prescription to let me live and eat like a normal kid . . . and see what happens. Our family physician, Dr. Andrew Klepner, knowing my mom and dad were near exhaustion, said, "Look, to give you guys the morning off once a week, why don't you send Scotty skating with my kids?" It was November 1967, and a new skating rink at Bowling Green State University had just opened. Dr. Klepner's daughters, Pam and Sandy, had just started a kids' skating class on Saturday mornings.

My parents, as much as they loved me and as much as they wanted me to get well, could not restore my health. They knew that if I had even the slightest chance at overcoming my illness, at saving my life, it was a fight I would have to win by myself, for myself. It was a hard lesson, a profound lesson, but ultimately the one that turned my life around.

A MIRACLE CURE?

Given my painful introduction to skating on the neighbor's driveway, my parents and I were—safe to say—reluctant to take up his offer. But Dr. Klepner insisted, "He'll be fine. It's just skating, let him just learn how to do something and interact with other kids."

So that's what I did. I showed up, tube dangling out of my nose.

The other kids, of course, said, "Eww!" upon seeing my plastic feeding tube snaking out of my nostril. Even so, skating turned out to be a lot more fun than it was four years earlier, when I fell backward, hit my head on the driveway, and insisted that I would never skate again. In fact, I soon discovered that skating was something I could do as well as the other kids.

At the time, other kids would pick me last for everything. I was always the smallest and weakest kid in class. I was different because I couldn't eat with the other kids because of my restricted diet. I wasn't allowed to have birthday cake or ice cream. I wasn't even allowed to have milk in my lunch box. I was just different. But I didn't like being different. So when I started skating, I liked it a lot because it was something I could do with other kids and also something I could do at my own pace. I could take as many chances as I wanted without some other guy inflicting his overpowering strength or athleticism on me. I tested myself and found that I really enjoyed it.

My parents kept me in it. I grew stronger. My stomach settled down and my lungs, which had been filled with phlegm, began to clear up. My overall fitness level improved, and I felt stronger. Within a few months, my feeding tube was even taken out!

The moist, cool air of the rink seemed to soothe my lungs, and my physical symptoms gradually started to dissipate. My parents felt they'd found a miracle cure.

I even started growing again, and it was amazing. The difference was night and day. My mom would say, "Oh, look how big you are growing! Your legs are getting so long!" And I'd say, "Oh, Mom, cut it out. That's so embarrassing." But I loved being fussed over. I loved how freeing it was to be on the ice, knowing that I was getting better and better. I loved knowing that I could finally do something as well as the other kids.

I kept going to skating lessons every Saturday, and soon the coach told my parents that I was good enough to start taking private lessons. It was a new feeling, participating in a physical activity that I wasn't losing in a competition to someone bigger, stronger, or faster than I was. It was just me and the ice. Me testing myself and learning at my own pace, seeing what I could do. And time just flew.

It was great to have a focus, a repetition, a challenge. *Hang on the wall; step away from the wall; hang on the wall; step away from the wall.* I wanted to learn how to skate forward, how to stop, how not to fall down, how to skate backward. The repetition took my mind off my problems, and for the first time in my life, I felt happy. Everyone has the potential to find something they enjoy as much as I loved to skate, and if they do, it can transform their lives.

> Everyone has the potential to find something they enjoy as much as I loved to skate, and if they do, it can transform their lives.

During those Saturday lessons while I was learning the fundamental skills of skating, the coaches made it fun. If I started to get bored or bumped my knee, they would try to make me laugh. I loved getting that extra attention.

Another thing I liked about skating was the girls. There was a pretty girl named Tammy Edwards who was involved in the program, and I really liked her. One time I fell and almost completely knocked myself out, but instead of quitting and running away in tears, I got back up on the ice again because I didn't want to cry in front of her. In that way, skating helped me learn how to deal with my mistakes in a responsible way. And something about simply going to the rink day after day helped me eventually overcome my fear of falling.

There was the play aspect of skating, which was really enjoyable. You would play tag, or you would see who could do this jump or do that turn. And then there was the competitive aspect of skating where you could try to do it better than everybody else.

All of the things that brought me to skating and kept me coming back for more—the things about skating that made me happy—are the same types of things that can make you happy in your own interests or hobbies. Think about it: why do you do that hobby or sport or activity? Chances are, the simple pleasure of the activity itself helps you reach that healthy place of happiness. As we get older, we perceive some things as more complicated than they really are. Even today, I am training to get myself back into good enough shape to perform again. Some days I feel like there's no way I can get my fifty-year-old body to do all the spins and jumps I did when I was young. But when I start seeing the glass half empty, I step back and realize it's just skating. I've done this before. My body remembers how to do everything; I just have to not let my mind get in the way. Sure, my body is less flexible, and my jumps aren't going to be quite as high, but because of my years of experience, skating is not overwhelming for me.

LEARNING HOW TO GET UP

I think back to my first days of going to the skating rink. It was so simple back then: all I had to worry about was not falling down. And I got better at it with each session. But it all started with the simple act of going to the rink, day after day.

In skating, the first thing you learn is how to get up from a fall. Trust me, you will fall. It's as certain a fact as it will be freezing in northern Ohio in February. Coaches teach you how to get up: first, push up on all fours like a dog, then kneel on one leg and push yourself up with your hands to standing. It's not that hard. In fact, it is easier to get up than it is to skate. So why fear falling?

It saddens me that a lot of people don't try new things because they're afraid of falling, whether literally or figuratively. It's a shame. As long as you know how to get up, you have nothing to worry about. It doesn't matter what the challenge is—athletics, business, romance, health, academics, the arts—the rule for getting up is the same: you just get up!

> It doesn't matter what the challenge is—athletics, business, romance, health, academics, the arts—the rule for getting up is the same: you just get up!

Then, once you learn to move forward, skating coaches teach you how to wiggle your hips and move faster. It's a slow process, but as you learn, your body gets used to this movement over the ice. Once you're able to stand up, move forward, move backward, glide a little bit, and stop, now it's time for your blades to leave the ice—little bunny hops, toe spins, pivots, and other tricks.

For a lot of my friends, skating was one of many sports they participated in, along with soccer, kickball, baseball, clarinet lessons, and other activities. They would skate for a while and then move on to other sports. But I was too sick to participate in most sports and activities. Skating was the be-all and end-all for me. It was something I wanted to stick with for a long time. I was growing taller and getting healthier. And for the first time, I had self-esteem.

Hundreds of kids all over America enroll in the kind of skating clinics I started in, but within a few years, participation dwindles. Often, after a few painful failures, kids move on to something else. The skaters who stick it out are the ones who get the double jumps, and the ones who stick it out through the doubles get the double axels and then the triples. The ones who become triple jumpers are the ones who compete at the higher levels and really get a lot of personal satisfaction out of the sport.

Usually there's some pain involved. Perhaps the skaters took a big fall and don't want to do it again. Or they think skating is too difficult and convince themselves that they will never get good at it, deciding they would rather be doing something else. Fear of falling, fear of failing—fear rears its ugly head at some point in any champion's life. Certainly, if you want to be a champion of happiness in your life, you will face some obstacles. But as actress Dorothy Bernard once said, "Courage is fear that has said its prayers."

I'm glad I faced my fear of falling and stuck with skating,

because, as grueling as the discipline and repetition of the sport often could be, it provided me good health, great personal achievements, and a renewed sense of self and purpose.

Landing My First Jumps

It was while skating that I had my first taste of the kind of happiness one can experience when setting a goal and working hard to achieve it.

I went from attending only Saturday morning classes, to going to the rink a few times a week, to taking private lessons. In skating, once you get to the next level of proficiency, you advance to the next level and then the next level—and you keep advancing for as long as you're motivated and interested. Once I was in private lessons, I started learning the whole testing structure, such as how to do basic figure eights.

In addition to taking private lessons, I would also free skate in public sessions, often playing games of chase, crack the whip, and tag. Some people say these games are reckless, but they do build skill. It's learning disguised as fun. Your skating is getting better and becoming more structured while you are having fun playing the games. Having fun kept skating interesting for me. You always have to keep things fun. If you don't, no matter how many awards you win or how much money you make, you will never be happy.

In my first summer of learning to skate, coaches David and Rita Lowry came to Bowling Green and took over the skating program, bringing with them skating coaches from all over the world.

It was an amazing summer. A brand-new skating rink in a university in northwestern Ohio had all of this phenomenal talent training. It was pretty cool. I met a lot of coaches, and not only did I get to be around other skaters similar in ability, but I also got to watch older skaters whom I held in awe. One of them was Jimmy Disbrow, who later became the president of the United States Figure Skating Association. He was a great guy and someone I always respected.

Scott Lowry was the son of David, the head coach at the rink. Scott was my age, my level, my everything. He even had the same name! Scott and I were friends and competitors. We were pretty close in ability though he was probably a little better than I was.

At the end of the summer skating school, we were eligible to participate in a big competition: the Bowling Green Invitational. It was my first performance competition. In a matter of weeks, I had to learn a minute-and-a-half routine, choreographed to music, and perform it in front of judges. Only four skaters—including my friend, Scott, and me—entered the subjuvenile division. But to me, it might as well have been the National Championships!

The music I had to skate to was "Italian Street Song." I got my first skating outfit, which was kind of a one-piece jumpsuit.

I remember stepping onto the ice for the first time alone for the performance. The dozens of times I had practiced my program were during practice sessions when the rink was full of people. But there I was—on the rink I'd skated on a few hundred times—all by myself. I remember my heart beating out of my chest as I was standing there at center ice, waiting for my music to start, and the judges were staring at me. I was so nervous and scared to be out there in front of the crowd, the judges, the other skaters.

As an almost-nine-year-old all alone on an NHL-size rink, the ice sheet looked gigantic. Now that I'm grown, the arena, which then seated about twenty-five hundred people, seems really small, but back when I was a kid, it seemed huge. It might as well have been Madison Square Garden.

My program started with three consecutive waltz jumps. Waltz jumps are the most basic of jumps, simply half-revolutions. Going forward, you jump from your left foot and rotate a half turn, counter-clockwise, landing backward on your right foot. You then rotate forward by stepping back to your left foot. I knew that once I got through those three waltz jumps, I would have the hardest part behind me. Landing the waltz jumps was the key to a good program.

> You can look for opportunities for happiness by dedicating yourself to the basic principles in your chosen field.

The music started and, with my heart racing and my legs feeling weak, just as I had practiced with my coaches, I began with a few bunny hops. Then I began gaining speed leading up to my three waltz jumps.

First jump . . . second jump . . . third jump. I did it!

The crowd applauded, and that calmed my nerves. From that moment on, it became exciting to be out there in front of all of those people performing the routines I had been practicing. I was no longer a sick, pathetic little kid; I was an entertainer.

When I ended the program, I had the biggest smile on my face. Nine months earlier, I had been a total beginner, clinging to the boards and falling down. But now I'd had my first taste of sweet victory, and I was hooked. I came in second, winning a silver medal attached to a blue ribbon. The medal is now on display in the World Figure Skating Museum and Hall of Fame in Colorado Springs.

Becoming a skater was a life-changing moment, not to mention a lifesaving experience, for me. I learned that once you take advantage of the opportunity to learn and experience and open yourself to a new way of living, you can't wait to do it again and do it better and find new ways of feeling that again and again and again.

Up until then, I had been defined by being sick. But in skating I found an activity I could do and enjoy. The purity of applying myself to the challenge yielded so much joy for me.

I think that is something everyone can do in every walk of life. You can look for opportunities for happiness by dedicating yourself to the basic principles in your chosen field. This is how you lay down the building blocks of happiness in your life.

Everyone has a different idea of what happiness is. What I did on the ice and in my career won't be the same as anyone else's version of happiness. Where I put my time and efforts and energies is different from anyone who came before or after me. Happiness is unique to you. You have to find what that is—and then know that you will definitely start by falling down.

Nothing can match the happiness you feel by doing something you love.

The Gold Medal of Happiness

My buddy, skater Steve Cousins, likes to say, "It is much better to be open to a result than to be attached to it." In other words, when we have no great expectations or outrageous demands, we can be in a position to be happy. But if your attitude is, "If I don't do this, then I have failed," you won't be happy. I have always been happiest when I was doing just as I did as a beginner skater, putting one foot in front of the other and progressing, having the attitude that whatever comes of it comes of it. That is what I love about Steve's philosophy of being open to results instead of attached to them.

> Make no mistake about it, being happy and fulfilled is all about the process.

In other words, as my mom used to say, "Do your best." In sports psychology this is called *paradoxical intention*. It's the idea that you train as hard as you can to improve and strengthen your skills, and then when the time comes, you don't worry about it anymore and figure it is what it is. You can thrive at your best because you've detached your ego from the process.

Make no mistake about it, being happy and fulfilled is all about the process. In skating, it's about training and preparing your body in order to do the best you can in a very stressful situation, so when that situation presents itself, the work has been done. You just let your body do what it's been trained to do. You simply allow those techniques and skills to kick in when you need them.

You know how to do it. You know the basic steps, and deep in your heart, you know what it's going to take. You just have to do it. You have to commit to seeing it through. And that is perhaps the biggest obstacle people have to being happy: they can't stay with the commitment.

So many people have a New Year's resolution of finally hitting the gym. The gyms are packed in January, but you can shoot a cannon through them in February when the excitement wears off. Happiness is a fundamental, spiritual commitment to dedicating yourself to the things in life that bring you the most joy.

That is why a lot of relationships fail: people forget they are committed. And when people end up feeling miserable in a job or other endeavor, it is largely because they have lost their commitment.

Commitment can be as simple as showing up and learning. Skating was a new activity that I enjoyed, and my parents liked it because they saw how skating improved my health when nothing else they had introduced to me had worked.

It started with my commitment to go to the rink and skate better than I did the day before. One day I could jump up and down, and the next I was learning to jump from forward to backward in a waltz jump. (You better believe that the first several times I tried a waltz jump, I fell!)

I had found something that gave me physical health and improved my self-esteem. Skating made me feel good emotionally, physically, and mentally. It was the first time I could commit to something that I enjoyed. Going to the rink on schedule, making skating a priority in my life, that was more important than anything else. To this day, no one knows exactly why skating seemed to cure my mystery intestinal illness, but if I had to put my money on it, I would bet it was because skating made me happy, thus making me healthy. In other words, being happy cured me.

Until I found skating, I lived life as a victim of my maladies. Many people also see themselves as victims and think that events in their lives define or limit them. Yet I've met others who have risen above their circumstances or perceived limitations to become better than they've ever been.

Things that happen to you may not be your fault, but they are thoroughly your responsibility. That sounds like a tough-love-lecture type of thing, but it's your life—no one is going to do it for you, especially the hard work. You have to do it for yourself.

So take charge of your life, commit to your goal, and before you know it, you will be well on your way to winning the gold medal of happiness!

CHAPTER TWO

Trust Your Almighty Coach

I am known as one of the most accomplished *individual* figure skaters. I have never competed in pairs. I often joke that I have never performed in pairs because I don't want to split my check in half, but the truth is that I am just not big enough to lift another skater and control her on the ice.

While I am best known as a solo artist, the secret to my success was that I was never alone on the ice. My faith in God—whom I like to call my Almighty Coach—was always lifting me to new heights I never could have reached on my own.

But it took me awhile to figure that out.

My personal journey to learning to trust all to the Almighty

Coach has been as twisting and complicated as an Olympic long-form program. And my relationship with God is, in many ways, informed by my experiences with the great skating coaches I've had the fortune of learning from over the years.

GOD-SCHEDULED OPPORTUNITIES

To a skater, a coach is like a god, especially in the sense that if you don't have faith in your coach—if you don't believe that your coach's message is the right one for you—you will not enjoy any great deal of success in the sport. I believe that my coaches, like everything in my life, were instruments of God's work.

In skating, the coach becomes a celebrity along with the athlete. The sport is so theatrical and so dramatic that the coach takes on a high level of importance. The coach makes all the big decisions. What your practice schedule will be. When you break in your skates. Your program, your music, and your choreographer. How much you train, how much you rest. Which competitions you enter, and which ones you don't. The coach is involved in every important decision for a skater. And the coach is usually also a manager, an agent, PR director, equipment manager, and psychologist. And coaches have a special importance in skating that they don't have in other sports. In football, basketball, hockey,

> My faith in God—whom I like to call my Almighty Coach—was always lifting me to new heights I never could have reached on my own.

or most any team sport, the head coach may get a lot of attention, but the impact is spread out over the entire team. A skater, however, has a one-on-one relationship with the coach. For that reason, it is a uniquely intense sports relationship.

My Christian faith has led me to believe that there is no such thing as coincidence. And I would include my coaches in that category.

My faith that God is always playing the Architect in our lives was hammered home by a sermon I once heard given by a law professor from Pepperdine University. The professor had never given a sermon before, but he was a committed member of our church in Malibu. Our pastor, Ken Durham, was away that weekend, and Ken felt very strongly that a church member should give the sermon in his absence. So he picked this law professor, who decided to preach about his belief that coincidence does not exist.

I will never forget how he got right up to the podium and told the congregation, "Coincidence is defined as a remarkable occurrence of events or circumstances without apparent cause or connection," and then he explained why he totally disagreed with that definition. As he saw it, coincidence was actually what he called a "God-scheduled opportunity."

A *God-scheduled opportunity.* When he said that, something clicked for me. All the seemingly random things—the highs and lows, the successes and failures, the loves found and lost, the life-threatening illnesses I had experienced and beaten down—suddenly didn't seem so random after all. Instead, I realized that all of these were God-scheduled opportunities—for growth, for learning, for self-expression, for living according to God's plan.

The late William F. Buckley, one of the most celebrated intellectuals of our time, said it best: "To believe there is no God is naive." When I began looking at the patterns in my life, I saw the events of my life as one God-scheduled opportunity after another.

Most everything that has happened in my life, even difficult things, has come from such a wonderful, beautiful place that I can't look back and say, "Wow, what an odd coincidence." Like how I found ice skating when I couldn't do anything else athletic or physical. There just *happened* to be a rink in my hometown. Bowling Green isn't a big place; there isn't much to do other than grow up, go to school, and leave. But there just happened to be a brand-new ice skating facility, a state-of-the-art rink that brought in world-class-level coaches, and I was given the fundamentals to learn and love skating—which gave me health and a second chance in life. There's no way that was a coincidence!

> When I committed my life to Christ, my faith changed my life in many positive ways and made seemingly unattainable goals—such as finding happiness—seem totally within my grasp.

Being adopted by two people who were willing and able to handle my unique health challenges and guide me through them is yet another example of the right thing happening at the right time.

When you start looking at everything that happens in your life as a God-scheduled opportunity, it is amazing how it not only brightens your outlook, but how it also infuses you with a greater sense of purpose, direction, and confidence. When I committed my life to Christ, my faith changed my life in many positive ways and made seemingly unattainable goals—such as finding happiness—seem totally within my grasp.

Searching for Love

In 2000, when I met the woman who would soon become my wife, it was hardly mere coincidence or luck. It was, as our minister so eloquently called it at our wedding, "divine providence." The fact that Tracie and I found each other at that time of our lives was so perfect, so God-scheduled, there is no way it could be chalked up to randomness.

I met Tracie about three years after I had been diagnosed with testicular cancer, and while I had succeeded in winning that battle, I was not happy to the core. Outwardly, I felt I always had to project joy and happiness, but deep inside my soul was hurting. I had just gone though a horrible breakup with my long-term girlfriend, and no matter how hard I tried to move on and be happy, I just couldn't.

I felt haunted—by disease, by past sins, by all the loved ones I had lost over the years. To my closest friends, I'd say, "Isn't it funny how I feel more comfortable in front of seventeen thousand people than one person?" I couldn't wait to get in front of any audience. I felt more comfortable in front of a crowd of total strangers, who were giving a level of love and acceptance, than I was being around the people who were closest to me. I felt more comfortable performing on the ice than I did anywhere else. You might wonder where I stood in my relationship with God. The best I can describe it is that I was searching, looking for answers. I would pray, tell Him thank You, thank You, thank You for giving me life, for beating back the cancer. But I would also pray and ask, "What am I doing? What is this all for? Where am I headed? Why keep me alive if I am just ending up so miserable?" I was confused, sort of lost, and I didn't know what it all meant.

I was grateful for the life God had given me, grateful for the love and acceptance I was getting from the people who were coming to the shows, and grateful for what I was able to do on the ice. But when I'd get off the ice and spend time with my Stars on Ice family, I knew I was failing with my closest friendships, and I didn't know how to fix those relationships. I always felt like people were more than willing to give to me, and I didn't know how to respond in a healthy way. I was more than happy to be the taker of all this wonderful attention and support from my friends, but I was entirely incapable of reciprocating.

Everyone has dark times. We battle diseases, we go through divorces, we grapple with self-doubt, and we cope with death. I was no different. I was competing well on a professional level. I was skating, working hard, and making a lot of money. In other words, I was doing all the things I thought should make me happy. But I felt badly about my failures. I felt like I hadn't been able to respond to the gifts I'd been given. I didn't know how or why, but I couldn't love others in a real, intimate way, and it just kept making me more and more miserable. I may have been superficially happy; I smiled through the pain, and I never lost my laugh. But in my private moments alone, with no one around, I was hurting. I was desperately searching for love—from God, from others—but I simply couldn't figure out how to find it.

After a while, living like this becomes toxic, not to mention isolating and lonely. In my search for happiness, I even went to psy-chotherapy. It helped me learn more about myself, but at the end of the day, I felt it was just a Band-Aid. I didn't feel that therapy was really the answer for me. Don't get me wrong; it definitely felt good to have somebody listen to me, and I know

> I couldn't love others in a real, intimate way, and it just kept making me more and more miserable.

many people who have experienced positive and lasting benefits from therapy. But at the end of the day, for me, therapy wasn't the cure I was looking for. It didn't shake me completely out of that funk and put me on the road to complete emotional and spiritual recovery.

About that time, through no coincidence, God brought Tracie into my life. We had met backstage at the Memphis performance of Stars on Ice. Tony Thomas, a mutual friend who had brought her to the show, introduced us, and I remember thinking what a nice and beautiful a person she was and how I had never before met anyone like her. But she was Tony's date, living in Tennessee, while I was doing my best to be alone in Los Angeles. Then a few months later, Tony and I were playing a round of golf in LA. He answered a call on his cell phone from his current girlfriend, and when he was done I asked him, "Whatever happened to that girlfriend of yours,

Tracie, from Tennessee?" He said, "Oh, we're just friends; we weren't dating." He then informed me that Tracie was in the process of moving to LA, and he would get me her number.

Soon after that, I went to a Fourth of July party. A friend of mine who was a caddy at my country club in Thousand Oaks said, "My cousin was going to come tonight, but she made other plans." And I said, "Okay, but I don't know your cousin." "Yes, you do," he said. "Her name is Tracie. You met her in Memphis last March."

I couldn't let this moment pass. Lightning was striking in the same place with the same woman, and I had a feeling the Man Upstairs was sending me a message. "Let's call her," I said. So right then I got on the phone and had a short-but-sweet chat with her. Three weeks later, we went on our first date.

I had all but given up on having a healthy relationship, and she'd kind of given up too. She'd stopped looking, and I'd stopped looking. But as we got to know each other, we really liked each other. I started by asking her to have coffee with me. She said yes, and afterward I said, "Wow, this is fun. We laughed a lot tonight. Do you want to have coffee again tomorrow night?" She said, "Sure." Then it was "How about dinner?" and then a movie. Our first movie date was an animated movie called *Chicken Run*. We just had fun together, with no pretense or any of the awkwardness that often comes with dating. From that great foundation, we built a solid relationship.

It wasn't until after our wedding that Tracie told me the truth about the night we met in Memphis. She was driving home from the show with her cousin Jeana, talking about what a great time they had. Tracie mentioned she had met me, and Jeana asked what I was like. "You know," Tracie replied, "Scott is the type of man I see myself marrying someday."

It was a God-scheduled opportunity. If Tracie and I had met each other two years earlier, our relationship would not have succeeded. I wasn't open to falling in love; I was closed off emotionally and physically. And so was she. But at the right time in our lives, when we were open to finding someone, God presented us to each other.

So often that is how it works in life. We try to force the situation. We think, *I need to do this,* or *I'm going to be this or that,* or *I need to be in a relationship regardless of how toxic or how horrible it is.* We tell ourselves we've got to make it work no matter what! In the past, I have thought, *I know we're two different people; I know we run two different paths and have nothing in common, but we kind of like each other, so let's find a way to make it work.* Well, that's not good. That's the opposite of good. That's trying to fit a square peg into a round hole. When I found Tracie, somebody so happy and positive and accepting, I began to be more open. I learned to become more loving and to share my fears, hopes, and dreams.

We didn't carry our emotional baggage from the past into our relationship. Rather, we decided that in order to form a healthy relationship, we had to let go of all that other stuff. It was as though we cleansed each other of whatever had happened before, and we simply started over.

Tracie not only taught me that I could open up my heart fully to another person, but she also brought me back in touch with God.

She started taking me with her to church. She was so committed to her faith, so strong in her relationship with God, that it inspired me to do the same.

During my loneliest, darkest times throughout the 1990s, I had isolated myself and (with the exception of my brief stint in therapy) had chosen to go off to the mountaintop alone and try to figure things out. We men often do that. We tend to draw back and turn inward when in crisis. It is probably hard-wired in our brains for survival, that caveman part of us that shuts off our emotions so we can go win the hunt. Problem is, we don't have to hunt anymore, so by closing ourselves off from others, we miss an opportunity to grow and learn and love. As God had done throughout my skating career, in Tracie He introduced me to just what I needed: a coach. She coached my spirit back to happiness again. I think we all need a friend—whether a spouse or a close friend or even a family member—to demonstrate love to us and help us along the way.

Discovering skating was similarly divinely inspired. Skating was presented to me, and I was able to act on it. I was so fortunate to find it. What other activity would appeal to my needs physically? What other sport would allow my body type to really thrive or would allow me to satisfy my desire to be the center of attention? I tried gymnastics, but for me, it was too structured, and I didn't enjoy the performance. Hockey? I tried it because all the boys thought skating was for sissies, but I was just too small. But I loved everything about skating.

You Can't Do It Alone

Skating is a great teacher of how to discover spiritual faith, because one of the first things you learn as a skater is that you can't do it alone. You need a coach you respect and trust; a coach who speaks your language; a coach you can relate to emotionally, intellectually, and physically.

I was blessed to have as my first coaches David and Rita Lowry. Mrs. Lowry made me laugh and made me enjoy coming to the rink all the time. But then they left to work in Buffalo, and I needed new coaches. My next coaches were Bowling Green college students. They were good, but I didn't feel I was learning enough.

When the Lowrys left town in 1970, I started taking lessons part-time from Guliano Grassi, a very strict taskmaster of a coach from Ft. Wayne, Indiana, who came to Bowling Green a couple of times a week to work with skaters. Mr. Grassi was good for me because he made me appreciate how good I had it with the Lowrys, who were far more nurturing as coaches. Mr. Grassi would stand in a long coat and bark instructions at me. His no-nonsense, disciplined approach came at a perfect time, as I was preparing for my first regional competition in the juvenile men's division. He was coaching me only part-time, however, and soon my parents and I knew it wasn't a good fit for the long term because I needed a coach who could give me full-time attention.

Before the regional competition had come and gone, I had hired a new coach named Herb Plata. Herb was a dynamic skater I idolized.

He had just begun coaching at Bowling Green. When Herb would skate, landing big axels and butterflies, he was an all-around pleasure to watch. He was a show skater, and more than anything else, I wanted to be a showman like Herb. Winning medals, coming in first, that stuff was all secondary to my desire to put on a great show to entertain an audience.

Herb helped me win my first qualifying competition, my first-ever first-place victory. He was a great motivator, someone whose showy style I tried to emulate. But Herb didn't focus much time teaching the compulsory figure eights that always caused me trouble and needed some work. Although I won regionals and was fourth at sectionals with Herb as my coach, by 1973 it became clear that I needed to train with a national-level coach if I were going to reach my potential. That would mean moving away from Bowling Green and training at a facility with better coaches and better skaters.

The place that made the most sense for me was just an eight-hour drive away—the Wagon Wheel Figure Skating Club, which was then located in Rockton, Illinois, a small city near the Wisconsin border. At the Wagon Wheel, some of the top skaters in the country were training under the direction of a man named Pierre Brunet. Janet Lynn, a four-time national women's champion, trained there, as did Gordy McKellen, who won the national men's title the year after I got there. The place was hopping; it was Middle America's mecca of skating at the time.

Pierre agreed to take me on, and my parents, as hard as it was for them to see me move away at age thirteen, knew it was the best thing for me. My parents made sure I was set up in school; a guidance counselor arranged for me to live in a dorm and made sure I had a compatible roommate; and Pierre and his coaching team took care of everything else. They looked after my skating sessions, my music, what I wore, you name it. It was my first taste of a world-class atmosphere, and I was intoxicated by everything Pierre offered.

Pierre Brunet and his wife, Andrée, were French national champion skaters and won two Olympic Gold Medals for pairs skating in 1928 and 1932. He would come to the rink every day, dressed formally in a white shirt, jacket, and tie, and he spoke with a thick, French accent. He did everything as classy as it could be done. He introduced me to structure and discipline in my skating for the first time. I responded very well to his coaching style. In my first year, I won regionals and sectionals, and then I competed in the National Championships, where I choked in front of a crowd of seventeen thousand people, falling five times. I came in dead last. I was physically ready to compete at that level, but psychologically I wasn't yet mature enough.

At that early stage in my career, I gave up total control to my coach. Pierre was like my brain. I didn't attend church in my teenage years, so I like to say that during that period of time in my life, Pierre was my religion. That's not to say that I hadn't been exposed to Christianity or been touched by it. I just wasn't ready to accept Christ into my life yet.

Janet Lynn, my fellow skater at the Wagon Wheel, was the leader of our group, and she was very committed in her spirituality. Janet would do everything she could to inspire everyone around her.

She invited us to church and prayed with us. She was—and is to this day—a very faithful Christian. I was very open to Christianity; I just didn't understand exactly how to do it, or in what structure to practice it. Plus, I was a teenager and had all the distractions common to teenage boys—girls, socializing, athletics. Janet and the churchgoing skaters all went to the same church down at Rockford. I went every now and then, on holidays, but I didn't commit.

As a young child, my parents took me to church. I went to Sunday school, sang in choir, and did all the things kids typically do in church. But once I started skating, pretty soon Sunday morning skating took the place of Sunday school. When skating kicked in to the next level, I stopped going to church altogether. My parents, seeing how inspiring skating was to me, let me blow off church.

As I developed as a skater, I became more and more a devout believer in the Church of Scott. Trust me, having a strong sense of my own individualism and being so focused and fawned upon during my adolescence, it was easy to join the church of myself. It was a great church! I could do whatever I wanted, skate as much as I liked, and be rewarded for it.

Also, like a lot of adults, I had grown somewhat disillusioned with the organized religion of my childhood because I saw how divisive it was for some people, and how some would put themselves above other people. I never lost my faith in God, but I did lose my faith in organized religion. I grew to resent organized religion. I had a real sense of spiritual belief, but I really struggled with the structure of religion. It wasn't until my courtship and my relationship with Tracie, and then finding Ken Durham and the Pepperdine University

Church of Christ, that I was finally able to disregard my pessimism toward organized religion and embrace Christianity.

FINDING THE RIGHT COACH

Until then, being a sort of rebel and focused on expressing my own individualism, I mostly saw how structure could be negative—in church and in skating.

I saw a lot of bad coaches. I am not talking about not-good coaches, but downright *bad* coaches who would be abusive and hit skaters with their skate guards, play all kinds of head games, even those who would walk away from the boards if their students didn't skate well. There are also great coaches who are like another set of parents whom you rely on for everything. Then there are situations in which skating coaches get in over their heads and end up teaching the skater at a level where they have no understanding. There are a few coaches out there who, when the skater gets to a certain level, are willing to say, "I've done all I can do; let's find the right person to take you to the promised land." But most don't. I saw way too much of that. I saw skaters getting abused, and it wasn't about learning and developing and growing anymore. The skater had become an extension of the coach's ego. A lot of coaches communicate this perspective to their skaters: you fail on the ice, you fail me. And I didn't want to have any part of that.

My disdain for self-interested coaches extended to church leaders of similar ilk. It is a shame, but I let my prejudice against a few rotten preachers keep me from participating in Christianity. And this went on until my late thirties, after my cancer. After I had gone through an unbelievable amount of difficult circumstances, Tracie came into my life with a real commitment to her church, to God, and to the teachings of Jesus. For the first time I felt like, "Whoa, I can do this."

Good coaches are good because they give their students the right information at the right time and let them take it from there. Since God is the Almighty Coach, He always has all the information right there in front of us at the right time. It's all there; we just need to open our eyes, minds, and hearts. It's amazing how many times you hear someone say, "You know, I was at a crossroads. I was really struggling, and I just picked up the Bible and I couldn't believe that it spoke to exactly where I was that day." Is that a coincidence? Not at all. Scripture will speak to you in a way that, if you truly understand it, will enhance your point of view and your life almost instantly. Because it's truth.

I think Proverbs 2:1–6 sums up the power and value of God's wisdom:

> My son, if you receive my words
> and treasure up my commandments with you,
> making your ear attentive to wisdom
> and inclining your heart to understanding;
> yes, if you call out for insight
> and raise your voice for understanding,
> if you seek it like silver

and search for it as for hidden treasures,
then you will understand the fear of the LORD
and find the knowledge of God.
For the LORD gives wisdom;
from his mouth come knowledge and understanding. (ESV)

Now, who you hear that wisdom from is very important. I've been to many churches, and I've heard all types of different styles of delivery and information. Some preachers are very old school, fire and brimstone, hellfire and damnation—and you know what you hear from some of the over-the-top televangelists.

> My long, winding journey to finding the right coach for me was not unlike my journey to finding God.

Then there are others who are more low-key, like my spiritual coach, Ken Durham, whom I adore and who has become family to us. Ken just gives you the information from the Bible for you to apply to your life and situation. Ken says one of the most remarkable things about Christianity is its conviction that Gods cares so much about us that He has, in Christ, come to meet us within our own history. History is both God's story and ours, together. And because God is so deeply interested in sharing our story with us, He has seen to it that everything we need to know—about Him, about each other, about ourselves—is right there in front of us.

The best coaches I have had approached skating in the same way. They gave me guidance, instruction, direction, and information then let me take it from there. In fact, my long, winding journey to finding the right coach for me was not unlike my journey to finding God.

TAKING IT TO THE NEXT LEVEL

While I was at the Wagon Wheel training facility, Pierre Brunet taught me so much. But Pierre was nearing the end of his career, and it became clear that I needed someone with a new perspective to guide me to the next level. After Evy and Mary Scotvold coached me to win the US national junior title in 1976, I had run out of money. I was eighteen and in my skating prime, but I was flat broke. Not seeing any hope, I planned to hang up my skates and go to college.

Back then, it cost about $12,000 a year to compete at a national amateur level. That was a lot of money, perhaps one-third of my father's annual income. I had no sponsorship at that time, and my parents were near bankruptcy. Nowadays, skating can cost as much as $50,000 or more per year. You have to pay your coach, pay for your living and travel expenses, pay a choreographer and a physical therapist, and you need money for costumes. It really adds up. If you don't have sponsors, you simply cannot compete at the highest levels.

Fortunately for me, in a very timely God-scheduled opportunity, world-renowned coach Carlo Fassi, who coached skating legends such as Peggy Fleming, Dorothy Hamill, and John Curry, learned of my dire straits and offered to coach me. Along with Carlo came a sponsorship from Chicago-area philanthropists and skating supporters Helen and Frank McLoraine. At that point, Carlo was by far the most successful coach in the history of US figure skating. I enjoyed learning from him, but after three years of being under his direction, I came to realize he wasn't the right guy for me any longer. It was a tough conclusion to come to, and it was even harder to work up the courage to tell him so and move on.

Carlo had helped me bring my skating to a higher level. Under Carlo, I learned the triple lutz and became the first skater to use it in the short program competition. Under Carlo, I made the World Championship team in 1978. But our relationship grew strained when Carlo began coaching Scott Cramer.

Scott Cramer was by far my biggest rival. So when Carlo decided to coach both of us, I was like, "Whoa, whoa, whoa! What's this all about?" My immediate reaction was, "How am I going to beat Scott if we are training with the same coach?" Carlo's response was, "I really want you both to do well." But that wasn't what I wanted or needed to hear. I wanted my coach to be 100 percent on my side, supporting me and training me. I felt betrayed and disappointed. Carlo's decision to coach both of us came at a time when I felt very vulnerable. I had just torn all the ligaments in my right ankle and was trying to learn the combination that Scott Cramer basically owned: a double flip–triple toe combination. You have to understand that doing the triple-second was something very difficult for a lot of skaters at that time. Now it's nothing. To do a triple-toe on a landing of any combination is pretty easy, but back then it was difficult for a lot of the established skaters to do that combination. Scott Cramer owned it.

And I knew that I wouldn't have a chance against Scott in the 1979 season unless I could perform that combination.

Before tearing up my ankle, I had finished eleventh at the World Championships and was ranked ahead of Scott Cramer. I was doing really well. So after the 1978 season, Cramer pretty much said, "If I can't beat him, I might as well join him," and asked Carlo to coach him too. The fact that Carlo accepted him was a shock to me. I understood it in a way because I think that Carlo, who was working out of Denver, always wanted his job back at the Broadmoor World Arena in Colorado Springs, the headquarters for US Figure Skating, and by having two of the top male skaters he could be regarded as the most powerful coach in the sport. I also had heard that a very powerful person connected to the Broadmoor World Arena had asked Carlo to coach Cramer. That would have meant a lot to him since the Broadmoor was the headquarters for the sport, and Carlo liked to play the politics of skating.

Having no other legitimate options for a coach, I went along with Carlo's split decision, as it were.

I don't harbor any ill will toward Carlo. But during that time that I had to spend every day skating on the same ice and sharing a coach with my biggest competitor, I was miserable. It was really tough to get up and skate every morning.

Carlo, as I feared, had spread himself out very thin between the two of us, and I needed extra training from other coaches, including a man out of Philadelphia named Don Laws. Don was helping out and got to know my sponsors, Frank and Helen. He showed that he had interest in my skating; whereas, Carlo didn't appear to show as much interest. I felt it was partially because I was damaged goods after my ankle injury.

That year at the National Championships, I skated well and came in fourth overall. But Scott Cramer skated his way into second place. I was officially playing fourth fiddle, and I didn't like it at all! After that, I spoke to Frank and Helen and told them I was thinking of leaving Carlo and taking Don as my coach, and they gave me their blessing.

So I went to Carlo and said, "I've established a pretty good friendship with Don Laws, and he's offered to coach me." I also told him that Frank and Helen would continue to sponsor me, that their support wasn't contingent upon being coached by Carlo.

> It was a pivotal moment in my career. If I made the wrong choice in coach, I might not progress to the next level.

"So what do you think? Do you want me to stay, or should I go?" I asked.

Carlo's response was, "Well, if you want to leave and go to Don Laws, then that's what you're going to do." He didn't beg me to stay. In fact, he didn't even *ask* me to stay with him. So, really, he had made the decision for me. And it was the right one for me.

Just three days later, I drove all the way to Pennsylvania to start training with Don at the Philadelphia Skating Club and Humane Society. It was a pivotal moment in my career. If I made the wrong choice in coach, I might not progress to the next level. But if Don was the right choice, then I could catapult to the next level: the Olympics.

A NEW DIRECTION

The first thing Don did was lay down the law. He told me, "You're going to work, and you're going to be disciplined. Whatever you do away from the rink is up to you. But it cannot affect what you do on the ice. If you're going to go out and whoop it up with your friends, don't let it show up on the ice. Because here on the ice, you're at work."

At that time, I was definitely a party boy. I'd work hard on the ice, but I'd play really hard off the ice too. I was twenty years old and was just out doing my thing, having fun. I liked my life away from the ice. I worked hard, and in all honesty, I played hard. I would drink a few beers and stay out late. I enjoyed joking around with friends and flirting with girls until the wee hours of the morning. I was like a lot of teenagers, especially ones living away from their parents!

Don told me, "I don't care what you do away from the rink." He knew if he went totalitarian on me, I'd probably rebel. So he said, "What you do is your responsibility. Just don't let it show up on the ice." It was the right message, at the right time, from the right coach.

Don was a handsome, well-dressed man. Even today, at seventy-eight, he looks the same as he did at fifty. He's an amazing man. He's well-read, intelligent, politically astute, and a very intuitive guy. He was president of the International Professional Skaters Union after he was president of the Professional Skaters Association. He is respected by his peers and liked by everybody who knows him. But until he agreed to coach me, he had never made the supreme effort of having a competitor at that level. I mean, he coached Reggie Stanley as a strong junior. He coached a couple of other guys who flirted with the top three, as well as senior men. But he had never coached anybody who could compete at the highest levels of international competition. Until me.

The first thing Don and I did publicly as pupil and master was an appearance at the annual Professional Skaters Guild of America conference. The group has its gathering in May each year, and that year it was in Atlanta, Georgia. During the huge banquet, I was sitting at a table when Don got up to speak. He said, "I'm sure you're all aware that I have taken on a new student."

My face suddenly turned red as a beet.

He added, "Just so you all know, there's a new direction, there's a new commitment, and there's a new philosophy." Those were his exact words. He continued, "We will not be a comedian on the ice anymore; we are going to be very focused and very hardworking." And he looked at me with that look that said, "Aren't we, Scott?"

I was flushed with embarrassment, but I knew why he did it. He was letting everybody know that this was the direction he expected me to take, and now I was going to have more eyes on me than I would have had he not made that announcement. He knew how to push my motivational buttons.

Plus, Don believed in me and was willing to give me all of his attention because he saw my potential. He gave me the road map, and I followed it. *Where do you want me? How much do you want me to skate? What days?* I let him guide me because I trusted him and his commitment to me.

Don kept me on a tight leash. He said, for example, "I never want your feet off the ice for more than twenty-four hours. I want you to be on the ice for a good stretch of time every single day." That was a brand-new thing for me. I'd usually take half of Saturday and all of Sunday off. Moreover, if I was having a bad day on Friday, I'd bail, not show up on Saturday. But with Don, I had to work through it no matter what.

With Carlo, I could miss the first few jumps of my program badly and still get to take the weekend off. But with Don, it wasn't like that. Instead, he would say, "Let's work through this, and we'll take another free skating session later this afternoon." Or "Get off the ice now; you're really off. Shake it off, go have lunch, come back, and we'll work on this in an hour."

The rest, as they say, is history. The following year I made the Olympic team, carrying the American flag at the opening ceremonies of the Lake Placid games. I then went from October 1980 through March 1984 without suffering a single defeat. In that stretch, I won four consecutive National and World titles and in 1984 won the Olympic Gold Medal at the games in Sarajevo.

Don was the perfect coach for me at that time. We were a truly divine pairing.

FINDING CONTENTMENT

I am a Christian, and contentment is the basis of Christian happiness. In Philippians 4:11, the apostle Paul says, "I am not saying this because I am in need, for I have learned to be content whatever the circumstances" (NIV). But that doesn't mean that I just let things happen to me. I changed coaches, changed programs, changed skating styles, and made hard decisions with each challenge God presented to me.

Indeed, I believe that God has given me everything, whatever the circumstances. He has given me money and taken it away, stricken me with disease and blessed me with health, given me victories and losses, good coaches and bad coaches. Through a lot of study and prayer, however, and the guidance of my pastor, I have learned how to be content and happy no matter what is thrown my way. Don't get me wrong. It is not a passive, fatalistic approach, but rather an understanding that I actively make the decision to be happy every day because I know that God is guiding me.

> I believe that God has given me everything, whatever the circumstances.

I have met five US presidents, countless CEOs of major corporations, world-class athletes in almost every sport, thousands of community leaders from across the country, and it's the rare person who finds true happiness without faith in something bigger than themselves. Whatever grants you strength beyond your own can empower you enough to make just about anything possible. It's the one great mark of all winners I've met in sports and business. Almost all believe they have a purpose scripted by God.

That's not to say that I sometimes don't get angry or frustrated or disappointed with the script that is handed me. But I have worked on enough television and movie sets to tell you that, like a good actor, it is our responsibility to make the best of what God has given us and to stay faithful to Him.

A DISAPPOINTING DIAGNOSIS

Perhaps the most disappointing script ever handed down to me from God was the one where I was diagnosed with a brain tumor. It brought me to my knees. Our son, Aidan, was just fourteen months old. Talk about bad timing for a God-scheduled opportunity!

It was a Friday. Tracie and Aidan had just arrived to see me host my annual fund-raiser for the Cleveland Clinic's Taussig Cancer Center. I wasn't feeling well and decided to meet with my urologist, Dr. Eric Klein. I'd had some blood work done a couple of weeks before, and the diagnosis was that my remaining testicle had kicked the bucket; as a result, I had very little testosterone in my body. That is what was causing my weakness and lethargy. Dr. Klein, who had been my urologist when I had cancer, said I could replace the hormone with gel and feel better in a few weeks.

> Even though so much is out of our hands, God is there to help us deal with any challenge.

But I wasn't satisfied. I asked Dr. Klein many questions. When I mentioned my blurred peripheral vision, he recommended I get an MRI on my brain. Later that day, I learned I had a brain tumor. I was shocked and scared more than ever before. How would I tell my young family that I had to deal with yet another health issue? Why me? How was this going to play out?

When my family arrived, Tracie asked, "Are you okay?" Not wanting to make a scene in public, I just said, "I'll tell you when we get back to the hotel." She instantly knew something was wrong.

A few minutes later, we were in our room at the Cleveland Ritz-Carlton Hotel. Aidan was crawling on the floor and playing with the phone, oblivious to his mommy and daddy's fear of the unknown. In a soft voice, Tracie asked me, "What's going on?"

I told her that they found the source of my lethargy, headaches, and lack of strength, and that they were pretty sure it was benign, but that . . . I had a brain tumor.

Tracie didn't flinch. She immediately grabbed both of my hands. Without hesitation, she bowed her head and started to pray aloud: "Dear God, help us. Help us find what's wrong, find a way to deal with it. And we pray that You will give us the answers we need."

I was so blown away, I started to cry. It was such a powerful moment. I realized that, even though so much is out of our hands, God is there to help us deal with any challenge. A few weeks later, I was baptized at our church in Malibu. I had finally accepted the Almighty Coach into my life, and it has made me the happiest man alive.

A Fresh Start

Many people, including myself before I became a Christian, have a hard time with happiness because they can't forgive themselves for things they've done in the past. And it drives them deeper into a whole other level of unhappiness. They can't let go of past indiscretions, past sins. I felt like that. I just couldn't let go of them. And it wasn't until after the brain tumor that I decided I wanted to be baptized.

I'd held on to all my horrible past situations, bad decisions, things I regretted, for years. But it was a crutch. I carried a darkness with me because I figured, *I'm flawed, and I did this thing wrong, or I hurt this person, or I did this, or I did that, and I deserve to be unhappy because of it.* I'd carry these regrets with me every single day, and I would suffer.

Becoming a Christian freed me of all that darkness. After my baptism service, Tracie asked, "How do you feel?" And the only word I could think of was "lighter." I wasn't carrying all those burdens of my past anymore. I was able to give them up, and I felt so much lighter and so much happier because I was able to forgive myself. It reminded me of the moments when Don Laws, or any of the great coaches I had, were the most helpful: when I made a mistake. The best coaches would say to me, "You made a mistake. It's over, it's behind you. You're not going to do that again. Let's move forward." Now God was coaching me, and my Almighty Coach's message was even more powerful and effective.

GOD IS ALWAYS THERE

If you're feeling terminally unhappy, the best advice I can give is to talk your problems through with God. Now, if you don't feel like you know God well enough to talk to Him, don't let it stop you from talking to Him—because He certainly knows you! Whether you want to call it a prayer or a conversation, just talk it out. There's no better therapist than God. And unlike a therapist or a private skating coach, God doesn't cost one hundred dollars an hour.

The act of talking to God is a first step in taking ownership and control over what's bothering you. If your unhappiness is based on somebody else bringing you down, somebody else hurting you, or somebody else making you miserable, just take that person out of the equation and focus on the relationship between you and God. You own it. This is your set of circumstances. Take ownership of it. Make it yours.

I hear people say all the time, "I felt like I was kind of off track. I just needed some guidance. Then I went to my church, and the minister spoke to exactly where I was at that moment!" This happens so often because we yearn for guidance from someone more powerful than ourselves, and God is always there to help us.

> A lot of people, including myself, have survived all kinds of difficult situations and have learned how to be happy.

Some people stick to the belief that their happiness is controlled by others—the abusive parent, a disease afflicting them, that horrible person at work. These people always see themselves as victims and never take ownership of their issues and take the steps necessary to heal. But I am here to tell you that a lot of people, including myself, have survived all kinds of difficult situations and have learned how to be happy. But it's up to you. It's your life, and you have to decide to take ownership of it and do the right thing. And you'll never be disappointed. This eventually will mean committing your life to Christ and going to a church. Of course, I'm not saying every church is perfect, but that's not the point. Church is just one of the many ways God gives us what we need to fight back the darkness and turn on a light in our lives.

It's amazing the difference God can make. You're going to be presented with problems—whether relationship issues, job stress, financial difficulties, or traffic—every single day of your life. All the information and inspiration, all the tools and support you need are there. All you have to do is just allow Him to guide you.

And that's what coaching is all about. It's guidance. The teachings of Christianity include spiritual coaching that helps you live the best life you possibly can. Trust your Almighty Coach, and beautiful things can happen.

CHAPTER THREE

MAKE YOUR LOSSES YOUR WINS

There is no delicate way of describing one of the cruelest facts of life, so I will just come right out and say it: life can really stink. Or to quote what some wise philosopher once said: stuff happens.

I think we can all agree that sometimes life just comes up all lemons. These sour sodas are fed to the rich, the poor, the good-looking, the not-so-good-looking, the famous, and the everyday unfamous. Bad things happen to people in huts in Bangladesh as well as those in Malibu mansions. There is no escaping the rough stuff of life. Many misguided substance abusers have thought they could dispose of their garbage through a drug or a drink or whatever vice gave them a temporary sensation of pure joy—only to find out that whatever they were seeking to escape was still there when they came off their trip. The truth is, we'd all like to live in a perfect paradise, that dreamy fantasy place where no one ruins our day, traffic is never bad, bosses never annoy us, bills never need to be paid, children never cry, spouses never cheat, the stock market never goes down, and you can do no wrong.

But, of course, there is no such place. Neverland simply doesn't exist. What does exist is another definite fact of life and a key to finding happiness: what you do with the uncontrollable junk in your life is totally under your control.

The 1980 Olympic Speed Skater Eric Heiden once said, "It's not the events in our life that define our character, but how we deal with them." Coming from an athlete who achieved the greatest individual Winter Olympic feat in history (an unprecedented five Gold Medals, including four Olympic Records and a World Record) at the Lake Placid games, I think Eric knows what he is talking about. And I couldn't agree more. It's how we *deal* with the things in our lives that creates our character. That is how you define yourself and figure out who you are.

I have learned firsthand how heavy life can be, and I have also experienced how hard but liberating it can be when you lift those burdens.

SURVIVING ONE LOSS THEN ANOTHER

When I moved to Los Angeles in the late 1990s, I was totally in a wilderness phase of my life. I wanted to get away from everyone. I had been given so many wonderful opportunities to perform for an audience—the Olympics, the World Championships, Stars on Ice—and I was grateful to be part of these events. But when I would step away from the spotlight, away from those professional achievements, I struggled personally. I struggled with decisions I'd made and the kind of life I'd been living, and I'd suffered through so many things. When skater Sergei Grinkov died at age twenty-eight of a heart attack, his death hit me hard. We were very close friends, and his sudden passing devastated me. And then the next year, I was diagnosed with cancer.

It seemed like one tragic thing after another. Friendships had gone away, relationships had failed, and I felt guilty. I felt guilty that I wasn't a better son to my father. I was always a mama's boy, and my dad basically died alone in the hospital while I was on the air broadcasting the 1994 Olympic Games in Lillehammer, Norway. I was working, of course. Why? Because I was always working! And I felt guilty about how my mother sacrificed so much for me but never got to see any of my greatest successes. I carried all this heavy stuff with me every single day.

> Although my fans might have thought I appeared happy and successful, the truth is that there was a huge portion of my life I didn't enjoy at all.

So although my fans might have thought I appeared happy and successful, the truth is that there was a huge portion of my life I didn't enjoy at all.

Don't get me wrong. Throughout my life, I was always trying to turn my losses into wins. But I had come to believe that no matter what level of happiness I found, I would soon be hit with a tragedy again. I was convinced that I would get injured, someone dear to me would die, I would get fired, I would be betrayed, or I would be stricken with yet another illness. I was riding an emotional roller coaster, and the lows were much deeper than the highs. I was just surviving from one doom to the other. I lived in fear of the next calamity that would strike me, which gave me a constant sense of anxiety and stress.

And then came June 2, 2002. The day when I realized I had been looking at the patterns in my life entirely wrong, that, in fact, I had been looking at the events of my life backward. And my life-changing insight came to me though the words of a thirteen-year-old cancer survivor.

INSPIRED BY A SURVIVOR'S STORY

Following my cancer battle, I did a lot of speaking engagements across the country, speaking at fund-raisers and various cancer charity benefits. Typically, I would serve as the keynote speaker and tell my story, hopefully inspiring others to keep up the fight and not let cancer win. That's exactly what I had been invited to do when I was invited to speak at the University of Chicago Hospital's Thirteenth Annual Cancer Survivors Day celebration.

Several hundred doctors and patients and their family members packed into a downtown hotel ballroom to hear from an afternoon's worth of speakers, with little old me, who had just gotten cancer into remission, being the last to speak. I normally would get nervous before speaking at these events, so, per the norm, I was pacing in the back, minding my own business and listening to the other speakers. Since it was a celebration, my goal was to keep my talk light and upbeat and deliver a pep talk to all the patients, caregivers, and family members. I couldn't have predicted what would happen next.

The speaker before me was a thirteen-year-old named Shawna Culp. Shawna, a competitive athlete, had lost a leg to cancer, but she confidently stepped up to the podium with a prosthetic right leg and barely a limp. She had a shock of red hair and an absolute glow to her. I stopped my nervous pacing and listened to this charismatic young woman.

> "The worst thing that ever happened to me is cancer. The best thing that ever happened to me is cancer."

Shawna spoke into the microphone and told the audience, "The worst thing that ever happened to me is cancer. The best thing that ever happened to me is cancer."

From the rear of the room, I could see just about everyone nodding their heads in agreement, connecting to her seemingly paradoxical statement. The place burst into applause.

There I stood, totally blown away by her words, by her incredible survivor's story. I was touched not just by that profound statement, but by everything that she shared that day—about the devastation initially of not being able to play sports, of losing her gorgeous head of hair, of having her childhood innocence ripped from her by cancer. But then she also told how she turned all those curses into the greatest teachers of the meaning of life, how cancer made her a better athlete, a better human being. In a five-minute speech that was probably the first of her life, she touched me in a powerful way.

Within a few years of that speech in Chicago, Shawna went on to play on the US Women's Wheelchair Basketball team as well as other competitive sports. She didn't sit around and mope about her tragedies. Instead, she turned cancer into the most positive force in her life. As of this writing, her cancer is still in remission. Shawna not only won that cancer battle, but she won the war that I hadn't yet won—that is, the war my mind was still waging with itself.

I don't even remember what I said to the group that day. What's for sure is that it was nowhere near as profound as Shawna's message. From that day on, I looked at what I believed to be "curses" as blessings, and I now realize that the ability to do so makes one a champion more than landing a perfect triple lutz does.

I had applied this outlook to my skating with some success. But when it came to my personal life, I had wallowed in self-pity. If I suffered a sore groin, I would look at it as a challenge, a positive motivation to overcome the pain and focus even more on winning. If I had stumbled on a landing, then during my next performance, I would see to it that I skated twice as well to make up for the error. I tried to live by Eric Heiden's wisdom—remembering that it wasn't the circumstances that defined me but my response to them—and it brought me gold medals and accolades and worldwide celebrity.

But while sports can be a great laboratory of life, it also is merely

a dress rehearsal for real life. I had a hard time applying those principles to my off-ice reality.

A NEW BATTLE TO FIGHT

In the spring of 1997, I was starring in the national tour of Stars on
Ice and had started feeling lethargic, nauseous, and just not quite
myself. My stomach hurt constantly, like a torn abdominal muscle
that just wouldn't heal and no amount of ibuprofen could alleviate.
So I had some tests done, and on St. Patrick's Day as I lay in the
emergency room at St. Francis Medical Center, resting my exhausted
body before a performance in Peoria, Illinois, the results came back:
I had some form of cancer. Dr. Jon
Carroll said, "We have found a mass.
We don't know if it is benign or malig-
nant. If it were me, I would take care of
this right away." Two days later at the
Cleveland Clinic, I was diagnosed with
stage three germ-cell testicular cancer and
a tumor twice the size of a grapefruit growing in my abdomen.

> While sports can be a
> great laboratory of life,
> it also is merely a dress
> rehearsal for real life.

I began my cancer battle with the kind of positive focus that I
had practiced on the ice all those years. I broke it down like a challenging and complex program that needed to be perfected, and I
was determined to win. This was my new battle to fight. I took leave
from the skating tour and headed straight to my arena of choice:
Ohio's Cleveland Clinic.

The diagnosis brought back memories of my mother and how

she bravely fought through her breast cancer with strength, humor, and dignity. I was just a teenager when she was diagnosed, and I watched her battle for three years before the cancer spread and finally took her at age forty-nine in the spring of 1977. She was working, going to school to earn her master's degree, and raising three children, while going through chemotherapy. I was a year out of high school, amid my quest to make the Olympic team, and her death absolutely devastated me. But some twenty years later, my mother's attitude—*I will fight this cancer to the death!*—now inspired me.

Mother set a great example, and I wanted to use every memory I had of her battle in my struggle. Even though she didn't win hers, I was determined to win mine. With the advancements in cancer treatments over the past twenty years, I knew that at least I would have the fighting chance that she never did.

> Some twenty years later, my mother's attitude—I will fight this cancer to the death!—now inspired me.

A week after the diagnosis, I was a patient at the world-famous clinic, beginning three months of intensive chemotherapy done in four rounds—five days on, sixteen days off; five days on, sixteen days off—until the chemicals destroyed the cancer cells. The doctors told me if my body could survive the chemical potion coursing through it over the repeated rounds, I had a fairly good chance of surviving. But, by the third round, I was ready to quit.

The treatment—daily IV injections of basically poison—was ravaging my body. Within a matter of a few weeks, I had gone from being in what I thought was the best shape of my life, performing in front of thousands of people every night and being surrounded by friends and my Stars on Ice family, to not having the energy to press the power button on the TV remote control in my hospital room. I was filled with chemicals that made all the hair on my body fall out. I was bloated and sick and worn down like never before in my life.

I already had a lot of practice at turning losses into wins in my life, but this was a challenge I wasn't sure I could overcome. By my third round of chemo, I didn't think I possessed the strength of character to overcome my cancer and was ready to call it quits.

> I already had a lot of practice at turning losses into wins in my life, but this was a challenge I wasn't sure I could overcome.

Like a runner in the Boston Marathon, I had hit the wall. That third round was my Heartbreak Hill, the incline at the twentieth mile that was breaking my spirit to the point of wanting to quit. More than that, I told myself that I was ready to die. That's what cancer does to you. It wants to break you down, tricks you into giving up just as the chemo has the cancer dying off and on its last legs. But at that later stage of chemo, it is not the cancer making you weak, but rather your chemical healing agent sapping you of energy while it beats down the cancer cells one by one. I made it through that third round on fumes and survived the fourth round only because I knew it was my last.

By the end of the last round of chemo, the doctors found no

evidence that the cancer had spread, and the tumor in my abdomen that just three months earlier had swelled to double the size of a grapefruit had shrunk to the size of a golf ball.

Six weeks later, surgeons removed the remaining tumor, along with my cancerous testicle, leaving me with thirty-eight staples down the middle of my body. Although the surgery rendered my ability to father children uncertain (and assured me that I would never win a swimsuit competition), it also cut out the cancer . . . so far.

CHALLENGES CAN BE A GIFT

I live every day knowing that today might be the day that my cancer returns. But rather than look at this as a horrific cross to bear, I call it my gift, a constant reminder of just how lucky I am to be healthy and alive. After all, what is joy without sorrow? What is success without failure? What is a win without a loss? What is health without illness? You have to experience each if you are to appreciate the other. There is always going to be suffering. It's how you look at your suffering, how you deal with it, that will define you.

> It's how you look at your suffering, how you deal with it, that will define you.

This truth was evident to me not only in the hospital but also on the ice. Without the humiliations, the losses, and the failures, the success I had in skating would have meant very little. Likewise, fighting cancer brought me tremendous pain, fear, anxiety, despair, and loneliness, and to come through that has given me an amazing perspective that reminds me of how precious and fragile life is. It allows me to appreciate the day. It is an odd blessing, and not one that I would ever choose, yet it is an amazingly powerful force that enhances my life. It is what survivors call the "gift" of cancer. Any challenge—be it romantic, physical, job-related, athletic, mental, financial—can also serve as a gift if we allow it to. Illness, like any setback, poses great challenges and immense rewards. It allows us to come in contact with a part of our being that we never would know existed without that battle.

> Any challenge—be it romantic, physical, job-related, athletic, mental, financial—can also serve as a gift if we allow it to.

I am no longer haunted by the image of swimming up to the surface and gasping for air, only to be sucked back down so I have to swim twice as hard to get back up to the top again. It's never too late to learn the lesson that every apparent curse comes with a blessing. It wasn't until I was forty-three years old and listening to a thirteen-year-old speak her truth that I realized my various roadblocks in life had been detours into a better direction.

This divinely scripted pattern goes back to the very beginning of my life when I was an unwanted pregnancy and was adopted by my parents. I went from being somebody's unwanted orphan to being a prized child who couldn't have had more love showered upon him. Then I suffered through my childhood illness, eventually discovering skating and being healed. Whenever I lost, I would find a way to win. I find that for every unbelievably horrible price I had to pay in life, something followed that was an equally great reward for responding to things the way I did.

Before Shawna's inspiring speech, rather than looking forward to the next challenge, I would dread it—despite the fact that things always worked out better for me in the end, that for every curse, there was a phenomenal blessing.

When I analyze my life experiences, the loss-turned-to-win pattern is undeniable:

- In 1977, I got Frank and Helen's sponsorship, but then my mother died. I followed her death with the best year of my budding career, making the World team in 1978.
- When I left Carlo Fassi—the coach who made me a national force—and switched to Don Laws, I was written off as going to a relatively unknown coach. But Don's commitment, coupled with our chemistry, took me to the highest levels that Carlo's did not.
- In 1981, my father suffered a stroke at the start of my undefeated run in competition. Rather than crush me, the stroke brought us closer and refocused my dedication to skating because I was determined to honor my mother and father. I translated the pain into success on the ice.
- Sergei's death, while a tragic loss, made me appreciate the beauty and fragility of life.

And on and on it would go, right up until today. Now I have two beautiful sons, Aidan and Maxx, to whom I am 100 percent dedicated with a passion fueled by my gratitude that I was able to father children despite surviving only on synthetic hormones.

Indeed, the apparent garbage of life has been dumped on me plenty of times, and it hasn't always been a health-related trash heap. For example, one of the greatest fears of many a working person is getting fired, and that's exactly what happened to me in 1986.

SUCCESS ON A SHOESTRING BUDGET

Right after my Gold-Medal win at the 1984 Olympics in Sarajevo, I turned professional when I was hired to headline the hugely popular Ice Capades, which started in the 1940s as entertainment during intermissions at hockey games and had grown into a global phenomenon, packing arenas with thousands of fans coming to see the best of the best in the ice skating world. I was signed to a two-year contract with a third-year option to be its main attraction. It was both an honor and a financial boon for someone who had toiled in near-poverty for years as I chased my amateur (that is, unpaid) dreams of Olympic triumph.

For two years, I dedicated myself to Ice Capades. I never missed a show and always skated my best. I did every publicity interview they asked me to do. Basically, I tried to make myself as valuable to the company as I possibly could. They were paying me good money, and I wanted to be the best company man I could possibly be. Then, out of nowhere, I was unceremoniously let go. The guy who had to tell me the news felt bad about it, but it wasn't his decision; the new owner didn't want me or my contract. When I asked what was the main reason for my dismissal, they said they didn't think audiences were drawn to male skaters and wanted to make a woman their headliner. They hired Canadian skater Elizabeth Manley after the 1988 Olympics to replace me. Ouch is right! Just two years after reaching my pinnacle, I was cast aside like yesterday's newspaper.

But what happened next marked another turning point in my life. Necessity being the mother of invention, I had no choice but to find a new job, and, with Bob Kain, my manager at IMG, we created a rival tour called Stars on Ice. At first, we ran it on a shoe-string budget and lacked the resources to wow audiences with eye-grabbing light shows and massive casts. But we let the talent speak for itself, and soon Stars on Ice had grown into a successful tour with major sponsors and massive audiences.

When Ice Capades let me go, I thought for a moment that my career was over. I was twenty-eight years old and washed up, not to mention a guy competing in a mostly woman's world of professional figure skating. Male skaters didn't sign big endorsement deals. Male skaters didn't headline shows. Male skaters either played second banana on tours or transitioned into coaching. I began to internalize the perception others had of me even though theirs was more driven by misguided financial reasons than by the actual fact that I was a one-of-a-kind talent. But within weeks of getting fired, I became determined to use the closing of that door to open a new one.

By 1995, Ice Capades had folded. Stars on Ice, for which I still serve as a producer, is now in its twenty-third season.

It's a good lesson for anyone going through a low point in their career. You have to look at it as an opportunity to do something else that will make you happy. People will come into your life and just let you down. Jobs will be lost. Relationships will end. You just have to know that it is probably for the best. Whether it is a romantic or business or an interpersonal relationship, sometimes things just don't work out. But life goes on and you have to be open to the next thing. Many times people get tied to the disappointment of what failed rather than focusing on the success that awaits them in the next opportunity. It is a fatal flaw for many.

> Many times people get tied to the disappointment of what failed rather than focusing on the success that awaits them in the next opportunity.

I have met so-called sick people such as Shawna Culp, who are beautiful and have the healthiest outlook on life I have ever encountered. I have met executives, kicked out of their companies and humiliated, who bounced back to even greater heights of success and happiness. Illness, setback, loss—they all touch your soul deeply and, if you let them, profoundly. All challenges are really just opportunities to learn more about yourself, to reach a greater understanding of self, of your mortality, and to be happy with that balance. Some people win the lottery and it ruins their lives. I've seen people reach heights of great fame and wealth only to fall into depression and negative behaviors.

Yet I've also seen people get cancer, and it enhances their lives.

I turned a growth-hormone deficiency, cancer, and a brain tumor into an advantage. We all will be dealt a bad card at some point in our lives. As Eric Heiden said, it's not what happens to you, but how you deal with it that defines your character. You can let it cripple you, smother you, and render you a despondent blob of flesh who can't get off the couch. Or you can turn it around and let it enhance your life and define it for the better.

Indeed, turning losses into wins is the mark of a champion.

CHAPTER FOUR

KEEP THE ICE CLEAR

Although most everything in my career worked out for the best in the end, I did not do everything perfectly. Far from it! I mishandled crises, made bad decisions, had to work hard to correct them, and failed to communicate my needs effectively. Too many times to count, I failed to communicate my feelings to associates, and it led to misunderstandings and hurt feelings. And the same can be said of my personal life.

The root of most of my mistakes was my fear of confrontation. To make people happy, I would try to accommodate everyone's desires even if it meant it would make me miserable. So when I would hit a bump in the road, I would often cave in to other people's wishes or demands because I wanted to please them. But by avoiding the confrontation, I would end up unhappy, and that ultimately made no one truly happy.

There is a lot of pressure that comes with trying to make everything perfect and make everyone happy. Pleasing others may seem like a noble, selfless pursuit, but when taken to an extreme, it is a recipe for unhappiness.

If I were better at confrontation, I probably would have been better at resolving problems instead of allowing them to linger and fester. I regret wasting a lot of time in my life repressing my true feelings or biting my lip when I could have been living more true to myself.

> Pleasing others may seem like a noble, selfless pursuit, but when taken to an extreme, it is a recipe for unhappiness.

That's where I got into the most trouble. When something or someone was making me unhappy, instead of standing up for myself I would just adapt to the situation because I didn't want a confrontation. In almost every case, I feared the fight more than I feared the consequences of not facing my differences head-on with people. I think a lot of people—especially those who, like me, were raised by nonconfrontational parents—practice this kind of conflict-avoidance life. The result is people take advantage of you, you lose self-respect, and in the end, you end up unhappy. If you don't keep the ice clear, you're going to get hurt.

Sacrificing My Own Happiness

My fear of confrontation negatively affected almost all of my romantic relationships before I met Tracie. I was good at starting relationships but really bad at solving problems, and especially bad at breaking up. When I knew a relationship wasn't working, I didn't want to deal with breaking it off. So I would stay in it, or I would check out emotionally. Instead of dealing with it, I would just go away. It was cowardly, and it created a lot of regrets because it wasn't fair to me and it wasn't fair to the other person.

I am still learning the lesson. As you have probably figured out from this book, I can be a slow learner. For a long time, I lived to be a pleaser, to make people happy, often at the expense of my own happiness. It comes from a place of not wanting things to go wrong, so in order to control things, I try to please others. To this day, I try to put somebody between me and other people when delivering news they don't want to hear. If somebody approaches me directly with a request, more than likely I'll do everything in my power to do what he wants me to do even if it's to my detriment. It wears you out. It just flat knocks you down after a while to live that way.

I am learning that I don't have to sacrifice my own happiness to make others happy. I am no longer the sickly boy, so vulnerable that he feels he must make everyone comfortable around him to preserve his own health and well-being. I am a man. Still vulnerable, by far not bulletproof, but yet an adult who has learned from the experiences of his life.

I see people sacrificing their own happiness like this every day in their personal and professional lives. They allow themselves to go down a road they don't want to go and then they regret it. They take jobs they don't want; they don't communicate when they're not happy; they stay in unhealthy relationships; they don't ask for a raise for fear the answer will be no; they harbor resentment and bitterness because they don't have the courage to confront people who have hurt or wronged them.

> I learned the hard way just how toxic it is not to keep the ice clear—to have open, honest communication about those things that bug you, hurt you, scare you—in your life.

I learned the hard way just how toxic it is not to keep the ice clear—to have open, honest communication about those things that bug you, hurt you, scare you—in your life. A perfect example of how I failed and then redeemed myself in this category was in the relationship with my longtime manager at IMG, the legendary Bob Kain.

SKATING ALONG IN THE RELATIONSHIP

In the early 1980s, as I racked up National and World Championship wins, I began to be courted by agents, managers, lawyers, and marketing experts, all of whom wanted to guide my career so that I could translate my on-ice success into business success. But I was resistant to bringing on an agent or business manager of this sort. As an amateur, I wanted to focus on what I did on the ice. International skating rules barred me from making money, so this decision was easy to put off. But after the 1984 Olympics, when I knew I was about to turn professional, I needed to find management.

IMG, the world's leading sports management company based in Cleveland, had been courting me for a while, but they didn't appear to be offering the kind of attention my career would need. But then in March 1984, IMG sent down one of their top guys, Bob Kain.

Bob was rising fast at IMG. He looked after Chris Evert, Bjorn Borg, and other top athletes. Borg was my favorite athlete at the time. I respected how he was able to keep his on-court focus while also maintaining a successful business career. He was a total role model. Bob visited me in Philadelphia just after the World Championships in Ottawa, which I won. We met in my lawyer's office, and Bob gave me the pitch on what he could bring to the table, how he would guide my transition from amateur to professional. I said to Bob, "Well, if you looked after Bjorn Borg, then I want to be on your list of clients." That was good enough for me. He was high up on the tennis division at IMG, and he was a guy on the rise. I could see that he was smart and that he was going to be around a long time. So instead of flying back to Cleveland, Bob spent the night at his brother's house in nearby New Jersey. The next day he was onstage with me in Atlantic City, announcing my retirement from amateur skating at a big press conference my lawyer arranged at the last minute.

Bob and I built a solid friendship and business relationship. He negotiated hard for me, and he did everything he could to get me into my professional years in a lucrative yet classy manner. We also had some great times together as friends. He helped me learn how to play golf (though I'm still learning), and we went to many different functions together. I have so many great memories of those early days. He was with me the day in 1984 that I threw out the first pitch at Yankee Stadium and then watched the game from George Steinbrenner's Owner's Box. That night, we attended a Rangers versus Islanders playoff game, which was the deciding game in overtime. The Islanders' Kenny Morrow, my friend from Bowling Green, scored the winning goal in overtime to eliminate the Rangers from the playoffs. It was just one of those days that was really fun. We had a blast and became close friends.

After I lost my job at Ice Capades, Bob created the Stars on Ice tour as a collaboration between IMG and me. Without Bob's loyalty and commitment, I wouldn't have made my professional comeback after getting fired from Ice Capades. In fact, I probably wouldn't be writing this book because you wouldn't remember Scott Hamilton.

As Bob rose through the IMG ranks, I began to sense that we were growing apart. He was promoted to senior executive vice president and could no longer handle my day-to-day dealings. My calls weren't immediately returned, and when we did talk, we hardly ever spoke about anything outside of work-related matters. Our golf games became fewer and farther between. I didn't understand what was going on with Bob. Before long, I began to resent the company. But, as was my usual practice, I didn't want to force the issue, opting instead to try to pretend it wasn't happening and just plow forward.

I suspected Bob's focus was elsewhere, on other, more lucrative clients, and instead of handling my career personally, Bob arranged for other guys on the company management team to work for me. By then, I was lumped into IMG's skating division, along with all the other skaters. Being a longtime veteran with an entire skating tour built around him, I wasn't happy being in a stable of many skaters; I didn't think it was best for me to be able to develop a successful career.

I may have been bad at confrontation, but I knew the lifespan of a professional male skater was not a long one, and I would have to cash in on my fame now because it would not last forever. There was a real sense of urgency and, frankly, an insecurity to my professional pursuits. Bottom line: I wanted to be their number-one guy. I didn't want to compete with other skaters.

THE LONG OVERDUE CONFRONTATION

The straw that broke the camel's back came in December 1991. I was in Denver for a Stars on Ice show, and Bob had come to pay a rare visit. It was opening night of the touring season, and I was wondering if IMG had arranged for me to compete later that winter in the World Professional Figure Skating Championships, a competition for pros that not only netted the winner money, but bragging rights as the world's top professional skater. It meant a lot to me to compete there.

I pulled Bob aside and asked him, "Am I doing the World Pros?" He responded, "I don't know."

Then he did something that, I am sure, he had no idea would upset me so much.

He asked Jay Ogden, the vice president of IMG in charge of winter sports, if I had a deal in place for the World Professional Figure Skating Championships. Jay said that he wasn't able to get me into the event at a reasonable price.

Well, first of all, I didn't want Jay representing me in a big deal like that; I wanted my longtime manager, Bob, to represent me. Don't get me wrong; I really liked Jay. And he was working hard on the phone every day with Dick Button, the event partner with IMG. It may have been naive on my part or just ego kicking in, but I wanted only Bob to handle those types of bigger deals.

Second, I was under the false impression that IMG was a 50 percent owner of the World Professional Figure Skating Championships and partially in charge of spending on skaters, so why couldn't they get me in at a reasonable price? At the time, that came across to me as a conflict of interest.

Last, and probably most important, the mix-up indicated to me that Bob was no longer in touch with what was going on in my career.

I relied on IMG for so much. They did my scheduling, negotiated the best rates for me, saw to it that outside employers took care of me the right way, and made sure I got paid on time. I started to feel uncomfortable that IMG, as a company, was owner of the Stars on Ice tour and, because of that, they may have had a conflict of interest in the sense that the tour was more important to them than any individual skater. This may or may not have been the case, but because I had allowed my communication with Bob to grow so poor and infrequent, I didn't know for sure, and it eroded our relationship.

Not being signed up for World Pros was a turning point. I was not happy about it. No one at IMG ever consulted with me about this decision. But instead of telling them how upset I was, I smiled on the outside while I stewed angrily inside. Rather than doing the World Pros that year, which I loved to do and felt was really important for my career, I did a small tour of Alaska. I performed in three cities in Alaska—skating for enthusiastic crowds whom I really appreciated, but nevertheless in relative obscurity. I was in great shape and skating really well, but I didn't compete in World Pros on national television. It broke my heart, and I felt IMG had failed me as managers and that Bob had failed me personally.

Instead of being confrontational, I allowed that anger to fester to the point where a month later I sat across from Bob and said, "You know, you're really not able to look after me anymore, are you?" And he answered, "No." So I said, "That's the reason I can't be with IMG anymore."

I didn't have the guts to tell him how miserable I had been with the way things had spiraled out of control. I only said that he couldn't look after my career anymore and that I wanted to part ways.

And so I left IMG. It was one of the hardest conversations I've ever had. It broke my heart much more than missing the World Pros that year. I could tell my decision took Bob by surprise because he didn't think it would ever get to that point. Nor did I for that matter. I had been avoiding confrontations like this all my life, but I was convinced I had no other choice.

While I am proud for standing up for myself, I am not proud of the fact that I let the IMG relationship get to such a dysfunctional place. I had allowed things to get bad. Instead of having the intestinal fortitude to handle my problems, I allowed things to fester and drive us apart. And it hurt my relationship with a dear, dear friend of mine whom I really respected and admired. Shame on me. I let my fear of confrontation rule my actions for so long that by the time I cleared the ice between us, it was not a satisfying exercise in self-empowerment.

I was sick to my stomach over it. Bob was stunned. He asked, "Well, where are you going to go?" And I said, "I don't really have any plan right now," explaining that I was just probably going to have my attorney organize and run things, that I wouldn't have a manager. Further complicating matters was that, due to my agreement with IMG for Stars on Ice, I could possibly lose the tour if I took on outside management. And since Stars on Ice was the best thing going for me, I didn't want that to happen.

A TOXIC SITUATION

Right before the 1992 Olympics, which I was broadcasting for CBS, my decision to leave IMG became public. Unfortunately, it was very bad timing for them. IMG had just signed Kristi Yamaguchi and were aggressively recruiting other top skaters. They feared that by losing their top skater, other firms would use that against them and be able to sign clients IMG wanted.

During the Olympics, the management team at IMG was upset with me. They proposed that we maintain a loose affiliation. I told them, "I think it's better that we just make a clean break, and we'll see how it works out. I might be begging on my hands and knees in a year to be back as a client. But for now, let's just break it off."

Rightfully, they were upset with me.

All this played out like a skating soap opera. After the Olympics, I went back to the tour, and even though I was still with Stars on Ice, Bob didn't want to have anything to do with me. He was hurt and embarrassed and felt that I had betrayed him.

> Instead of having the intestinal fortitude to handle my problems, I allowed things to fester and drive us apart.

It was a bad scene all the way around. It really hurt our friendship, and my enjoyment of the tour suffered for the next year or so. The situation between IMG and me finally got to the point where the atmosphere became very toxic within the tour. Here was a situation where the star of the tour (that being me) had a totally unhealthy relationship with the owners of the tour, and the tension was so thick that you couldn't even cut it with a chainsaw. I was skating the best I'd ever skated in my life, was in great shape, and was putting on amazing shows for huge crowds. But the rift between IMG and me was tearing me up inside. It finally came to a point where I couldn't take it anymore.

FINALLY CLEARING THE ICE

Going into the 1993 season, I set up a meeting with Bob. I flew to Cleveland and sat across from him, and I just laid it all out. Then he told me his side of the story, and we both got pretty emotional. It was always more than a business relationship. He explained how he had always been looking out for me, but as he rose in the company and took on more of a managerial position, day-to-day contact with clients was no longer realistic or good for the company. He also said that had he known how upset I was at his apparent inattentiveness, he would have stepped in sooner to try to repair the wounds; he would have better explained why he moved me into the skating division of the company rather than keeping me on personally.

> I wasn't communicating, and everything suffered because of it.

Bob was right. I wasn't communicating, and everything suffered because of it.

I had finally come to clear the ice. To show how much I meant business, I wore a jacket and tie into his office that day. Bob knew that the only times I ever wore a tie were for funerals or weddings!

At Bob's invitation, I ended up staying at his house a couple of days. We went to his son's baseball game, played some golf, had dinner, and resurrected the friendship. We hardly talked business. I'll never forget Bob telling me, "I'm always going to look after you and make sure IMG represents you well. I won't let this happen again." And I said, "That's good enough for me."

At the end of our time, he said, "Let me think about this, and we'll figure out the best situation possible for you."

After a few months, I called him and asked, "What's going on?"

He said, "I still think the best thing for you is to be in our skating division."

"What about Kevin Albrecht?" I asked, referring to an IMG agent I respected who was in the Canadian office.

He responded, "I never thought of Kevin."

I said, "Kevin would be someone I would really enjoy."

So Bob said, "Let me talk to him."

A few weeks later, I was in Bowling Green doing the Skating Club Show, and Kevin flew down to see me. He spent the day with me, and he said he'd love to look after me. From then on Kevin was my manager, and Bob and I remained business associates and close friends. Bob and I played a lot of golf, and he stayed involved in Stars on Ice. With Katarina Witt, Kristi Yamaguchi, Kurt Browning, and the whole gang, business was booming, and our friendship had been restored. All because I manned up—better late than never—and cleared the ice between us.

> Business was booming, and our friendship had been restored. All because I manned up—better late than never—and cleared the ice between us.

A few years later, when I found out I had cancer, Bob was the first person I called. He was the one who made the necessary arrangements for me to be treated at the Cleveland Clinic. When I married Tracie, he was one of my best men. And he has always been the first person I consult when I have a serious business decision to make. When he retired from IMG in 2005, he said that he would remain in an advisory role for two clients: Chris Evert and Scott Hamilton. He said, "These are the two people I really want to make sure are taken care of." Bob's retirement signaled my departure from IMG as well. But he made sure that I had a smooth transition once I decided on a new manager. Bob created the positive momentum needed in my newly formed management relationship with Larry Thompson. After everything we had been through together, his parting gesture was touching beyond words.

COMMUNICATING WITH OTHERS

Whenever you are experiencing tension or frustration in a relationship, whether at work, at church, in your neighborhood, or even in your own family, I highly recommend saying something that for too long I failed to say. Next time something or someone is bothering you, just say, "Look, here are my issues. Let's talk about it." For many years, I was afraid of confrontation and allowed things in my personal and business relationships to get totally out of hand. When you "communicate" in silence, when you feel like something is happening but you're not really sure what it is and you just sit there and stew about it, it takes

> Next time something or someone is bothering you, just say, "Look, here are my issues. Let's talk about it."

on a whole other identity and becomes a bigger problem than it actually is.

I know friends who are having marital problems. They think, *We don't really talk anymore; we don't really do this anymore; we don't have the same type of passionate relationship.* All of a sudden, this disconnect takes on a whole other level of significance and eats away at the bond between you and your partner. Pretty soon, you're screaming at each other from down the hallway about who is going to take out the garbage. Without communication, you lose the love.

I see people in my life who are going through this very problem in their marriages, and it is sad to see. Sure, I repaired my relationship with IMG, but if I hadn't, life would have gone on. But when it comes to marriage, there is a lot more at stake than 15 percent of your earnings. Your children, your family, and the sacred bond of marriage are at stake.

I've talked to friends who say, "I'm struggling with my marriage, and I don't know what to do." Or "You know, my wife is doing all this stuff with the kids, and I am working and traveling. And the next thing you know, my spouse, my best friend in the world, is telling me, 'You have no idea who I am anymore, do you?'" That happens all too often. We all change, every day. Every day we have a new experience; every day we have something that happens that alters us inside. If you don't share it, if you don't put it out there, you create room for a division.

Whenever I hear a friend relaying these kinds of communication problems in his marriage, I think how much I don't ever want that to happen to me. And that's a big reason for writing this book. Beyond the fact that I'm an optimist, I don't want people to make unnecessary mistakes like I did. I have lost friendships because I didn't talk problems out. Looking back, I suffered through a lot of miserable years, a lot of the really tough years that sent me into my self-imposed wilderness after my cancer battle. And 99 percent of my pain was a result of my not being able to muster the strength to communicate effectively things that were upsetting or hurting me. It created a level of misery that I could have avoided had I just been strong enough to communicate what was going on in my heart.

I still have those issues. I'm sure there are misunderstandings still out there between others and myself. I'm sure there are people I work with professionally who carry a level of uncertainty or resentment toward me. It's my fence to mend, even if I didn't break it all by myself. And to this day, I still struggle with pleasing people. I'm getting better, but I still struggle with it. I'll just say, "Oh, it's my fault." Or the biggest cop-out of them all: "It's not you. It's me."

Now, I'm not saying that you should grab somebody by the neck and shove him into a corner and force him to listen to you. Rather, go to that person and say, "Here's what I'm feeling," and discuss the issue. I realize there's a popular assumption that men are going to stay in their cave so don't bother talking to them about feelings, and that's one way of looking at it. But I think even men will listen if something is presented with love, support, and respect, regardless of how horrible it is. If you approach someone with "This is how I'm feeling," without saying, "You made me feel this way," the discussion opens up communication that will take away all those things that are divisive and destructive and horrible. You must take ownership of your faults to make it right. You have to be willing to be honest and authentic.

Connecting with Audiences

As a sports entertainer, my job is to put on a good show, which often means sparing the audience the knowledge of what might be under the surface. I did a show in Madison Square Garden in 1994 after I had buried my father earlier that same day. My job was to make sure that my pain was not visible to the audience. They came to escape their troubles, not to be drawn into my own pain.

> If you aren't authentic in what you do and say, you won't enjoy much success.

There is another side to this. When competing, from the moment you step on to the ice to the moment you walk off after your postprogram interview, you are being judged by the audience. I think one reason I struggled with being myself off the ice was that I had trained so hard to be a certain character in my performances that it bled over to my real life. But the more experience I got, the more I realized that the best performer was usually the most honest performer. If you aren't authentic in what you do and say, you won't enjoy much success, because audiences want to feel like they are connected with you in a personal way.

I learned this lesson from Doug Wilson, the television director for

ABC during my time with the Olympics. He once asked me, "You know what's as important as your performance?"

"What's that?" I replied.

And he said, "Your interview. The audiences at home are going to see performance after performance after performance. They're going to see a lot of amazing and wonderful things, but what's going to set athletes apart is how they connect personally, as individuals, with the viewing audience. What you say and how you present yourself at the Olympics means as much—or more—than your performance."

The more I thought about that, the more I realized how true that is. You can watch the greatest athletes in the world performing, doing what they do best in their Olympic disciplines, but if they don't connect with you, their performances become one-dimensional. There's no depth or meaning to it.

> If you tell it like it is, it's amazing the connection you can make with people.

When I was competing, television stations often put together profile pieces about athletes. A lot of them were tearjerkers about a certain tragedy or injury that an athlete had overcome. Audiences soon became desensitized to these tragedy stories leading into what the announcer would always call "the most important performance of their lives!" Many of these stories seemed forced, a bit contrived. Audiences are savvy and can see right through that kind of thing. That's why I always tried my best to be honest and not create something that wasn't there. I wouldn't give interviews where I played up my childhood illness in some over-the-top emotional way because that wasn't how I viewed it. Why fake it? The audience—whether in an arena or watching on TV—knows when someone is real and when it's being manipulated, and that perception can backfire on a skater. But if you tell it like it is, it's amazing the connection you can make with people.

A WINNING STRATEGY

This approach paid off for me in the wake of my 1984 Olympic performance. Truth be told, I didn't skate my best at Sarajevo. I did, however, *train* perfectly. I didn't want to look back and say, "If I only had worked harder that Monday in October or that Tuesday in November, then I probably would have done better here today." I didn't want any regrets because I knew that the pressure was going to be enormous and that anything could happen on the ice. I could cut a bad piece of ice, catch a rut, step in a hole from a previous skater, or pull a groin the week of the competition. I mean, I've seen so many things go wrong for skaters that I wanted to control everything I could control. That meant making sure I was skating my compulsory figures perfectly. That way, it would serve as an insurance policy just in case something went awry with my freestyle performances.

In Sarajevo, I did my compulsory figures perfectly. I couldn't have done better. I did three different figures, and they were the most perfect lines I had ever skated in my career. There was not a single mistake, not a single line that didn't match perfectly with the other. They were perfect eights. In fact, when I look back at them now, I think, *I have no idea how I accomplished that.* They were that good! (As Muhammad Ali would say, "It ain't braggin' if it's true.")

But when I got to my short program, the adrenaline was so much that I couldn't land a jump in the warm-up, and I had to quiet the crowd because they were going crazy. I was just insane with adrenaline. It got so bad that after I finally landed a couple of jumps at the end of the warm-up, I went down to the locker room and looked in the mirror and screamed at myself for a while just to get rid of that adrenaline and extra energy. I wanted to wear myself out a little bit so I could perform.

When it came time for the performance, I got through the first two jumping passes without a problem. But then the adrenaline kicked in again, and I skimmed the wall on one of my footwork sequences and followed that by executing one of the slowest camel spins in the history of the Olympic Games. It was not even juvenile level; it was so bad. All I was trying to do was just force the rotations out so I wouldn't get a deduction. But it was so pathetic that it was embarrassing. Don Laws still teases me about it to this day: "Oh yeah, your Olympic camel spin, is it still going on?" It was that slow.

When we finished the short program, the scoring came out to be a tie between me and Canadian Brian Orser. Through the scoring rules, the tie was broken in his favor. But I knew that since I had won the figures by a mile, I didn't have to win the short program to take the gold. That was my strategy. I knew that if I won the figures, I only needed to finish in the top three in the short and long free-style programs. Given Brian's scores, in fact, I knew that as long as I came in no lower than fifth in the long program, I could still take the gold. In other words, all I had to do was not mess up!

The day came for my long program. It was the biggest performance of my career. A worldwide television audience was watching to see if I would, as expected, win the Gold Medal or choke. I'd been fighting a cold and wasn't in the best condition that day. I was standing in my position, sweating right through my outfit, telling myself, "Do not blow up. Just get through this. Calm, stay calm, stay calm."

The music started and, like all my performances, I started with a triple lutz, which I landed perfectly. The next jump, however, was my trouble jump: the triple flip. Rather than doing three rotations, I only did one. My left leg, which was supposed to be close to my right leg, had whipped out from my body, and I couldn't complete the two other planned rotations. I'm thinking, *No! I just popped a triple flip in the Olympic Games. This is not happening.* So I tried to smile it off. I thought, *Okay, okay. You made your mistake; you haven't done that in months. Just finish your program.*

I went on and hit everything else. I was going into the last minute of the program and was starting to have trouble with stamina. I wasn't breathing very well and felt a little off balance, and I ended with this wonky, goofy-looking Salchow. It was probably the worst long program I had done in years, even in practice. I hadn't even practiced one that badly in probably three months, and that was my Olympic performance. Brian went out after me and literally skated the most perfect long program I had ever seen. But when it came down to the scoring, I came in second place in the long. So by virtue of the cumulative points in the figures, short and long, I won the Gold Medal.

At the press conference afterward, the media couldn't resist asking about the white elephant in the room: that I didn't skate very well but won the gold.

"Well, what did you think of your performance?" a reporter asked.

"You know, it's probably the worst I've skated in months," I replied. "It was probably the worst I skated at this level."

The reporters wouldn't let it go. "Do you feel like you deserved to win even though Brian Orser won 70 percent of the competition?" a reporter continued.

"Absolutely," I said. "I came in here with a strategy. And my strategy was this: win the figures and come in top three in the free-styles. No one else will be able to place in the top three in every event. And if I'm able to do that under this scoring system, then more than likely I will win the Olympic Gold Medal.

"I did not skate well. But I came prepared to win under the system, and my strategy won, and I won under the rules. So, yeah, I deserved to win."

My response probably wasn't the most expected answer to give in front of a throng of international press. Some public relations guru or image handler would have told me to be more humble and just give credit to Brian and thank the judges and the crowd and not come right out and tell the truth. Poor Doug Wilson was probably in the ABC production control room, screaming, "No, Scott! Just shut up and go home!" (Then again, he might have been very pleased that I was making good TV.)

A few days later, I was flying back to the United States and was on the same plane as sports columnist Woody Paige. Woody is a tough guy, known for his biting sarcasm and his distaste for athletes who give pat answers. Woody walked up to my seat and said, "You know something? I gotta tell you. Before the press conference, I had my column written on you, and I was gonna rake you over the coals for winning the gold even though Brian skated better. But I tore it up after your press conference because I've never seen an athlete be as honest as you were, saying, 'Yeah, it was not pretty, and, yeah, you probably will have an issue with me, standing here with the Gold Medal around my neck, but here's why I deserve it.' You were right. And I wrote my article all over again. I just wanted you to know that I completely appreciated your honesty."

> The truth can be the best thing to say even when it is unpopular.

That experience taught me that the truth can be the best thing to say even when it is unpopular. It is better to be unpopular but genuine than popular but inauthentic. If you try to sweep something under the rug, or if you try to sugarcoat something or try to tell it halfway, it's still fake. But if you're speaking truth and say, "That's the way it is. Sorry if you don't like it," then people will respect you.

That's where we struggle right now in so many businesses, and even in politics. So few people are willing to stand up and say, "All right, I screwed up. I didn't think this thing out. Given all the information I had at the time, I thought I was doing the right thing, but you know what? Maybe I made a mistake." It seems like no one's ever willing to do that. They think admitting your mistakes shows weakness. I think it shows greater strength to stand up and take responsibility. Not only does the public respect you when you tell the truth, but the truth also sets you free.

TELLING THE TRUTH

As I have said, however, I can be a slow learner. I also have always found it easier to be honest in front of millions of people than one-on-one. It is interesting that throughout my skating career there was probably no depth of physical pain that I wouldn't have put myself through to achieve a goal, but at the same time I went out of my way to avoid the pain of confronting people with my feelings if I feared it would upset them. But I have gotten better at being as honest away from the rink as I am around the rink.

For example, I was very fortunate that I was able to repair my professional rift with IMG because when I needed them, they were there for me. As I already mentioned, when I was sick with cancer, the first person I called was Bob Kain, and my agent Kevin Albrecht was in my hospital room every single day as I was getting chemo. I will always love Kevin for that. And it almost didn't happen because I wouldn't share my feelings with Bob. But because I finally decided to be honest, we were able to get past the hard feelings and grow closer. When I needed those two men the most, they were there for me.

Your own life is surrounded by people like Bob and Kevin. Trust them to understand you even if you fear that what you are feeling will jeopardize the relationship. Trust me: clearing the ice by telling the truth about how you feel will make your relationship stronger than ever.

CHAPTER FIVE

Think Positive, Laugh, and Smile Like Kristi Yamaguchi

I have been called a showboat, a sellout, a cancer glorifier. I've been told I was too short, too bald, and too goofy to win a gold medal. My critics haven't left any label unused in their efforts to rain on my parade. You name the put-down, the insult, the attack, the mud, and I have had it slung my way.

When this happens to us, we face the temptation to descend to our critics' level and give them an "eye for an eye." We can even cite Scripture verses to justify our tit-for-tat counterassaults. But while doing so might make you feel better for the few seconds it takes to dump on those who dump on you, I assure you that in the long run, it will not make you happy.

If you don't like football fans, why would you go where football fans go? You wouldn't. You would avoid them like the plague. So then don't venture down the nasty highway of negativity on your way to nowhere. You might have a troublesome coworker you wish would leave, but the more you wish it, the more the opposite happens. Don't go there. Once you start using your critics as tools for positivity and self-growth, you'll no longer be controlled or affected by them. Rather, they will become an inspiration for your motivation and happiness.

> What's the best response to someone who's trying to make you unhappy? Be happy.

What's the best response to someone who's trying to make you unhappy? Be happy.

RISE ABOVE NEGATIVITY

I am not the first person to implore others to resist the temptation of focusing on the negative, the darkness, or what we Christians call the devil. In fact, in James 4:7–8, we are told, "Submit yourselves therefore to God. Resist the devil, and he will flee from you. Draw near to God, and he will draw near to you" (ESV). Many Christian pastors and writers have expressed the benefits of positive thinking.

Every day of your life, something or someone is going to throw something at you that will challenge your ability to rise above negativity. An illness, a death in the family, physical exhaustion, a bad day at work or the loss of your job, credit card debt, someone cutting you off in traffic, or even a lack of manners can throw you off. But you have to remember in these trying moments that it isn't the events in your life that define you; it's how you deal with them.

Every time I was thrown a curve, I had to find a way to deal with it. I don't know how I was able to do it sometimes. I just know that each time I was faced with something, I would try to find the positive side and, when appropriate, the humor.

Take, for example, being short. I don't need to list the infinite number of negatives about being far shorter than your average man. But on the positive side of things, I can tell you that at five-foot-four, I don't take up as much space. I fit in airplane seats more comfortably. My clothes don't require as much material, thus helping save the planet (and I am a better environmentalist since I don't use as much water in the shower!). I can even shop in the boys' department, where everything is cheaper and just the right size.

On the ice as a youngster, judges would tell me how being short would keep me from competing with taller skaters who would present a better artistic and technical impression. Instead of letting their negative outlook rule me, I found I could create an illusion of size on the ice and did. I had to exaggerate every movement, jump higher, rotate faster, smile broader. And it worked. As such, every time I would step up on the top of the medals podium, I would be eye level with the taller skaters on the step below me and appreciate the view from there better than I would looking up in defeat.

I strongly believe that the only disability in life is a bad attitude. The more I live, the more I realize just how true that is.

LESSONS FROM MY MOTHER

No one taught me this lesson better than my mother. In 1975, when she was diagnosed with breast cancer and went through chemotherapy, she did it with humor and optimism. Having been through chemo myself, I can tell you how she coped with it was amazing. She always tried to keep it light. She didn't want us to be stressed out or scared, so she would say things like, "Oh, finally, I have a reason to quit smoking." When her hair started to fall out, she didn't try to hide it or wear a wig. Instead, she cut her hair short and joked, "What a relief that I don't have to spend so much time fixing it in the morning." And when her hair completely fell out, she said, "Now I really don't have to worry about bad hair days. Maybe I will finally go blonde!" When she couldn't eat and lost a lot of weight, I remember her telling me, "I've lost all this weight. Isn't this great? I could never do this before!"

My mother brought so much humanity and humor to each challenge throughout her cancer experience. Trust me, if you can exhibit grace and elegance while coping with chemo, you can look graceful falling down on a triple toe loop. She really tried to take the high road—that positive road we all know is the path to happiness—not only to help herself, but to take a lot of the fear and the anxiety away from her family.

Remarkably, even after the doctors removed her left breast, she came back with a prosthetic one she kept in her bra. I remember her one time holding it up in front of our family and joking, "What do you think? Not bad, eh?" She passed it around the table like it was a turkey cutlet and had us all laughing. She had the ability to deflate any seriousness that would creep into the mood. She didn't want any of us to be sad since it would make it even harder for her to remain upbeat.

My mother kept everything light and filled with humor. She showed great courage and optimism and never an ounce of fear or dread or victimization. Of course, she wasn't happy about having cancer. There's no way in the world she could be happy going through all the pain and suffering that comes with breast cancer. Nonetheless, she handled it in a way that didn't spread the disease to us. In doing so, our home environment remained healthy and productive and forward focused. No matter what kind of pain she was in, she kept us happy no matter what.

She set such a good example for me. Of course, I had no idea that twenty years later I would be in a similar fight for my life with testicular cancer, but her example was the one I followed. She taught me how to act in a crisis. Not by telling, but by showing—and that's almost always the most powerful, enduring message. She was my role model, and I'm hoping that the way I handled my chemotherapy set an example for someone else going through it. And in that way, the attitude is passed on. Sometimes that's the only way you can really give back, by paying

> Sometimes that's the only way you can really give back, by paying it forward.

it forward. You can't pay it back to the person who gave it to you. That's impossible.

As a skater, I learned these lessons earlier than most people. Mostly because the first thing you usually do when you try a new jump is fall flat on your behind. Not only is it humbling in a healthy way, but it teaches you that falling and moving on is just part of the process.

But it was all due to Mother that I fought cancer the way I did. I decided I would handle it with humor, dignity, and courage. I wasn't going to allow anyone who brought negativity or pity to be in my close circle. If you couldn't make me laugh, you were going to have a hard time getting close to me. There just wasn't room for anything other than, "You're going to be just fine. This is just a bump in the road." Some may criticize me for being too Pollyannaish or unrealistic. All I know is that this secret has gotten me through some of the scariest, darkest days of my life.

My perspective was, "Okay, I've got cancer. I've got to do something about it. All this stuff goes on hold now. I have to deal with this thing now. So how am I going to deal with it? Well, I'm going to surround myself with people who make me laugh. I'm going to surround myself with people who are optimistic and nurturing. I'm not going to surround myself with people who will hold my hand, crying and saying, 'How could this happen to you, of all people?'" If it wasn't helpful, I didn't want it in my life. I needed as much positive energy as possible to beat my cancer. If it works for cancer, it can work for any of the far lesser challenges you face on a daily basis.

The Positive Power of a Smile

Sometimes you can get things moving in a positive direction just by smiling.

About ten years ago, I was on the Stars on Ice tour with Kristi Yamaguchi, one of the all-time greats of women's figure skating. I was the veteran skater, while she was young and fresh off her Olympic win. Kristi taught me an enduring lesson: the power of a smile.

I remember one performance in which she leaped into a triple lutz only to slip on the landing and fall smack on her behind. I mean, this wasn't just a regular tumble. This was perhaps one of the hardest falls I had ever seen. And if you don't know what Kristi looks like, let's just say she doesn't have a lot of cushion to fall on. It looked like she could have broken something.

> Sometimes you can get things moving in a positive direction just by smiling.

Falls happen all the time, and pro skaters know that you get right back up and continue your program. But the way Kristi bounced back from her fall was unlike any I had ever seen: she hopped up almost as soon as she fell and, through it all, was flashing the biggest smile. It was just an awesome, beautiful, genuine smile. The kind of grin that so belied her error that even I wondered if in fact she had just fallen. Why? She didn't let the mistake ruin her performance, the rest of which she performed perfectly. Instead, she sold the crowd on the smile—not the fall. In fact, it was hard to remember the fall at all. After her program, I asked myself again, *Did I see what I think I saw?*

It is an amazing lesson we can apply in our lives. Recently, when Kristi appeared on the ABC reality series *Dancing with the Stars*, she would smile through even the hardest dance routines. She had practiced years of smiling despite on-ice wipeouts. I was so proud to see her doing the same on the dance floor.

In life, when we knock the proverbial snow off our butts (getting rid of the evidence) and move forward with a smile, we have already succeeded. A smile not only tells everyone else you're fine, but it also convinces you that you aren't going to dwell on the mistake.

> Any situation can be turned around into a positive.

The worst thing you can do is sell your mistake by standing up, brushing the snow off your behind, and taking five seconds to get back into your routine. The best thing you can do is bounce up as quickly as you can and pretend the fall never happened.

If you don't sell your mistake, people aren't going to focus in on it. And neither will you. I've noticed a lot of times when I'm watching skaters in a performance and they make a mistake, if they bounce right up and go about their business as if nothing ever happened, it's not important to me. But I've seen skaters who fall within the first minute of their programs and then in their bows, they pretend to put a pistol to their heads, or they roll their eyes, clearly showing disappointment in their performances. When I see a skater do that, I think, *Why would you just sell a panel of judges your mistake when the other four minutes were pretty phenomenal?*

You can take this approach with everything you do. Let's say your boss gives you a big assignment to give your company's presentation at a convention. The day comes, and you are standing in front of a few hundred people, wanting so badly to impress your boss, and you realize that you forgot to upload half the slides in your PowerPoint presentation. What do you do? Well, you don't focus on the error, that's for sure. You focus on all the good material you did prepare, and present that. And look on the bright side: without the other slides, your presentation may go faster and prevent half the crowd from falling asleep midway through your talk. Any situation can be turned around into a positive.

THE HARDEST JUMP IS AFTER A FALL

I have always said in my television commentary that in skating, the hardest jump to perform is the next jump after you have fallen. Because your confidence is shaken, your timing is probably a little bit off, and you're rattled. The only way to not fall again is to let go of the mistake so you can land your next jump. The same is true in life, especially when it comes to maintaining healthy relationships.

I'm at an age where people can get a little bit antsy or unhappy about their marriages if they think things didn't turn out the way they planned. Maybe their spouse cheated on them, or they didn't make enough money and aren't providing enough security, or the kids have been less than angels and they feel like failures. So many people hang on to the mistakes, hang desperately on to the problems, as if focusing on them will in some miraculous way make them go away. They will focus in on everything that's wrong with the relationship rather than focus on the positive things. Those are the marriages that will fail.

I was out to dinner a long time ago, and an older man told me that he and his wife were celebrating their fortieth wedding anniversary. I asked what was the key to his marriage lasting so long, and he said, "Let me tell you. Here's the wisdom I live by: the key to a long-term relationship is having a short-term memory." He was making a joke but at the same time making a profound point about what makes relationships work. You not only have to let go of the past problems but you also have to be able to laugh at them.

> I'm a big believer that smiling—and its first cousin, laughter—can get you through the toughest times.

I'm a big believer that smiling—and its first cousin, laughter—can get you through the toughest times.

The same day I was diagnosed with cancer in 1997, I had an evening performance in Peoria, Illinois. Fearing that it could be the last show of my life, the show took on more meaning than any single show ever had. I decided that if this cancer was going to take skating, and perhaps my life, away, I was going to go out with a bang. I went out and did the opening number without a hitch, doing a triple toe loop, two double axels, and, of course, my patented back flip. It was a flawless opening routine. I then went out for my first solo performance and hit two triples, two double axels, and another back flip to a full standing ovation. There is no way anyone in that crowd could have guessed that I had just been diagnosed with cancer, and I was proud of that. In fact, I thought, *Wow, I am really good at having cancer!*

But I still had to perform my second-half routine, an emotional program set to the weepy ballad "I Who Have Nothing." As I started my routine, the emotions of the moment began to overtake me and I was fighting back tears, trying hard not to let sadness keep me, from pulling off the performance. As the ballad got even weepier in mood, all these horrible thoughts kept creeping into my head to the point where I was just not present. Worse, my next big jump was my toughest: the triple lutz.

As I passed along the boards on my acceleration into the jump, I caught a glimpse of a woman in the front row, putting on makeup. A very attractive lady, in the middle of what I deemed the most important performance of my life, was putting on makeup. She was staring into her compact mirror, completely consumed by making sure she looked good. She couldn't care less about what I was doing out there. And I just started to laugh to myself. This intensely emotional moment turned so light and funny to me. The anxiety and fear and emotions of just hours earlier being diagnosed with cancer melted away, and it gave me the levity to pull off the triple lutz. The folly of this woman not caring at all about my serious performance gave me a lightness that filled me with a sense of power and determination. If you start looking around, you, too, will find things that can lighten your mood when you're pulled into the darkness. It may be a jogger with a dog who looks just like him, a humorous bumper sticker, or a cute little boy pretending to be Superman. You can find something humorous; you just need to look for it.

You have to find humor in life no matter what comes your way. It isn't easy, but it is the best way to go. If you take a broken piece of glass and turn it in the light, you can make a rainbow.

LEARN TO FORGIVE YOURSELF

Stress is toxic. Worry never accomplishes anything. And, most times, things take care of themselves. Instead of wallowing in self-pity about my seemingly lifelong string of ill health, I like to say that I just have a hobby of collecting life-threatening illnesses. It is always best to, when given the option, keep things bright.

When in front of an audience, I would try to keep people engaged no matter what I was doing on the ice. When people make that commitment to come to a show, I want them to know that I appreciate it fully. If you have a tough show, have a couple of falls, get trippy, or stumble through choreography, no one will really care as long as your total effort is there and you are enthusiastically displaying joy every step of the way. You will be forgiven for your mistakes in this life, as long as you are willing to forgive yourself.

> You will be forgiven for your mistakes in this life, as long as you are willing to forgive yourself.

Some people are drawn to skating for its moody, dramatic side. But I went into skating to entertain and make people smile. I believe that when people go out, they really want to get away from their problems. They want to experience something that will take them away. I was never interested in going out there only to show off technical skating or political skating or something thought-provoking or esoteric or beautiful. I just wanted to give people a pleasant escape.

That's why from very early on in my career, I put together programs that were humorous. Many people in the skating world deemed me an innovator because I brought a much-needed dose of comedy to an otherwise overly dramatic sport. But, truth be told, I ripped off a National Champion named Gordie McKellen. He was my hero. And without him, I don't know if I would have had the career I had because I wouldn't have been brave enough to go there with my comedic programs. I used to watch Gordie and see how he could hold an audience in the palm of his hand, and a lot of it was very funny. We actually did a routine together once for a show in New Jersey. It was to Spike Jones's "You Always Hurt the Ones You Love," and it brought the house down.

Gordie combined the humor of an ice show comic with the technical skills of a champion, and it was a thing of beauty. I wanted to get standing ovations not only for being good, but also for letting people know it was okay to come to the rink and laugh and have a good time.

Thanks to Gordie, a lot of my most memorable programs were comic ones. In 1978, I put together a routine to the tune "Short People," by Randy Newman. There I was, nineteen years old and all of five-foot-nothing, skating around the rink to this song that proclaimed "short people got no reason to live." The crowd just ate it up.

Another comedic program I did was choreographed to "In the Mood," by the Henhouse Five Plus Two. The song was basically the sound of chickens clucking. It was a fan favorite and became one of my signature numbers. Both those routines were choreographed by Neil Carpenter from Canada. Neil and I became good friends and laughed and laughed while putting those programs together. Sarah Kawahara and I did most of my professional programs together, including "Saber Dance." It's strictly a classical piece of music, but I did the last half of it in slow motion. The music's going crazy, and I'm trying to skate in slow motion. The joke of me being too slow to keep up with this ridiculously fast song never got old.

Another comedic inspiration for me was Freddie Trenkler, known as the clown prince of skating. I saw Freddie skate with Ice Capades when I was a little kid, and I was just in awe of him. I remember telling my mom, "I want to skate like Freddie Trenkler." His body movements and his ability to turn an everyday skating move into a bit of physical comedy with a twist of his hips were inspired. He was a genius. Freddie had a forty-year career with Ice Capades not because he was the best technical skater (far from it) but because he was funny, and it made all the difference in the world because the crowds loved him.

One could make the argument that comedy and humor gave me a career. Let's face it: with my, uh, *looks*, I was never going to be the shirtless stud on posters that girls would have hanging in their bedrooms. I was never going to be a *Teen Beat* kind of sex symbol. Women liked me, I suppose, but not because of my good looks. Since I was neither tall nor dark nor particularly handsome, I had to be accessible and do whatever I could to try to make people laugh. That's how I survived off the ice, and I wanted to take that on the ice. I thought if people were coming to see me skate, then I was going to put something in there that was clever, goofy, silly, or funny, and pretty much every program I did had an element of that.

I tried to do silly things as much as I could because I wanted the audience to have a good time, and I wasn't going to take myself too seriously. Art for art's sake is a great thing to do, and I applaud it. But a lot of the fine arts are supported by endowments, not by ticket sales. Professional skating is supported exclusively by ticket sales. Moreover, a true artist is really appreciated years after he's dead. I really didn't feel that a straitlaced technical skater would ever be remembered beyond his death. He might win some competitions, but his legend would fade fast.

> Since I was neither tall nor dark nor particularly handsome, I had to be accessible and do whatever I could to try to make people laugh.

LOOK FOR THE LIGHT SPOT

If you want to experience happiness and optimism in your life, then finding the humor in everything isn't a choice; it's essential. You've got to find the light spot, even in the darkness. If you don't, you can't be happy. There is so much darkness in the world, and it has the potential to suck you in like a black hole. Just as staring at a welder's flame will eventually make you go blind so, too, will looking at the darkest things in life all the time. God created the sun for many reasons, one of which is to give us light. Perhaps we have darkness so we can appreciate that light. You notice that we sleep when it's dark? I like to think this is God's way of saying, "Hey, guys. Don't pay too much attention to the darkness."

Scientists will tell you that laughing and smiling produces endorphins, hormones that can give you a feeling of contentment and even euphoria. These chemicals are stored naturally in the brain. It's up to us to bring them out. Everything from strenuous exercise to simply doing things that make us happy can activate endorphins.

The positivity muscle is something that you have to work on building up over time. From an early age, I truly felt I had no choice but to look at the humor. I was short, pale, skinny, and, for a few years, had a feeding tube in my nose due to my intestinal illness. Humor was the only way to defend myself on the playground. I would either get beat up or get out of trouble by disarming or charming somebody with humor.

> If you want to experience happiness and optimism in your life, then finding the humor in everything isn't a choice; it's essential.

Even if you are bigger than Shaquille O'Neal, it's healthy to find the humor.

Laughing can be the greatest cure for unhappiness in anything we do. In fact, there's no better testing ground for the power of laughter than in marriage. Getting the opposite sexes not to kill each other has to be one of God's greatest (and most comical) challenges. The same can be said of most jobs, families, and even most commutes down the highway. If anything, being your own favorite comedian is a good insurance policy against unhappiness. You know that at least someone will always make you smile.

You can employ this skill in how you respond to the generic greeting, "How are you?" Most people say, "Fine." My response often is, "Perfect. Never better. Best day of my life." It always gets at least a smile and sometimes a double-take. And when I am not in fact having a good day, it actually helps turn my day around.

A LIFE WORTH LIVING

A friend of mine went through a divorce not long ago. When he told me about it, I said, "I'm really sorry, because I thought you guys were really good together." He replied, "You know, people say life's too short. Sometimes life is too long."

I thought, *That's a shame. It's a relationship. Okay. It didn't work. Ultimately, you're a good person, and so is she. You'll be fine. But don't lose perspective and wish your life away.*

And that's why I think life is hard, but it's also great. Life wouldn't be worth living unless it was difficult. What's the point of doing anything if it's easy? It's so much more valuable when a challenge has to be overcome. You know how you feel the first time you walk into your first apartment. You know how you feel the first time you start your first car, kiss your first girlfriend. I mean, it's a rush of adrenaline, the feelings that you have, that almost takes your breath away. You're allowed to experience these things because you worked for it and earned it; it's yours, and it's something that you did on your own.

I find a lot of people are bummed out about dying. They fret over getting older, and some fall into despair over the sadness of having to leave the physical world. Of course, they need to find God, but they also need to adjust their point of view.

> Life wouldn't be worth living unless it was difficult.

Sure, a lot of being happy is taking time to smell the proverbial roses. But it's also about employing the daily discipline of not taking yourself too seriously.

LAUGHING AT MYSELF

I'm a movie junkie. My friends tease me because there isn't a comedy out there I don't find funny. I am a sucker for a good laugh. But while I made dozens of TV appearances over the years, I had never starred in a movie. That is, until *Blades of Glory*. The movie was incredibly popular and has grossed well over a hundred million dollars. I was glad that most reviews about my performance (playing myself) were favorable. But what nobody knows is that I almost didn't take the job because I had been taking myself too seriously.

Back in 2006, I was approached about playing myself in the satire. If you haven't seen *Blades of Glory*, and if you are a fan of Will Ferrell and can handle a little raunchiness, I highly recommend seeing it. If you are in the world of competitive skating, however, I *demand* that you see it! The movie is so biting, such a send-up of all the clichés of our sport, that seeing it will give a healthy dose of humor to our serious little world.

When I was first given the script, my immediate reaction was, *If I do this movie, how could I ever show up in church again?* It was pretty raunchy stuff. Then my second thought was that if I was part of a movie that mercilessly mocked competitive skating, I could be blackballed by the powers-that-be who take themselves far too seriously. But, honestly, my biggest concern was a selfish one. I had built a career based on a public persona that, while lighthearted, was an earnest, respectable one. I feared that doing a movie so out there, so self-deprecating and goofy, could erase all the hard work I had done over the years.

To be fair, the original script was insanely out there. The basic storyline is about two rival male skaters who get banned from the sport but are able to make a comeback as a doubles team due to a loophole in the rules that doesn't preclude men from skating together. If there was a joke on the edge, the writers took it all the way off the cliff. There were some things they wanted me to say as a TV commentator that I wasn't comfortable saying. But the producers worked on the script and toned down some of the scenes and dialogue enough to where I finally said, "I have to do this!"

Until then, I had always vowed that if I ever acted in a movie, I would play a character and not myself. I viewed it as being cheap to play yourself, but respectable to play someone else. Some of my handlers had warned me that, once you play yourself, it's game over for having a *serious* acting career. So I turned down dozens of offers to play myself in roles.

But when *Blades of Glory* came along, things had changed. First of all, I had just battled two life-threatening illnesses and, frankly, didn't care as much about what people thought anymore. I felt liberated. Second, Will Ferrell was starring in it, and at the time, there was no hotter comedic movie star than Will. Just the idea of Will playing an aging, boozing figure skater was hysterical. (Will has said that his character, Chazz Michael Michaels, was a cross between Clint Eastwood and Steven Tyler from Aerosmith.)

And the more I considered the movie, I realized that I wasn't so much playing myself as I was playing the director and writer's image of me. So while I would be playing "Scott Hamilton," the truth was that I was playing a tongue-in-cheek version of myself. And I had a blast doing it.

NEVER SAY "NEVER"

If you want to experience happiness in your life, never say "never." It's interesting to note that more often than I would like to admit, whenever I said I would *never* do something, I eventually ended up doing it. Take, for example, skating to opera. Early in my career, I had a distaste for opera and vowed I would never skate to an opera or ballet or anything too classical. I found that kind of music too dramatic and just the kind of conventional skating I was rebelling against. Well, a few years later I skated to "Figaro" and did it as a comedy. So I only half kept my vow. Then after that, I did "Don Quixote" as a ballet dancer and made it funny by playing it somewhat straight, grounding the humor in a legitimate choreographed routine. I was growing as an artist and a performer, and if I had stuck to my silly *never vow*, I would have lost the opportunity to grow and push my performing to the next level. That is why I would do an occasional ballad such as "I Who Have Nothing."

Having grown up in Ohio, I once declared I could never live anywhere but out West. Now I live in Nashville, Tennessee, and I couldn't be happier. After I went through a rough breakup with my girlfriend in the mid-1990s, I vowed I would never get seriously involved with anyone again. A few years later, I met and married the woman of my dreams.

> If you want to experience happiness in your life, never say "never."

I have basically waved the white flag and admit that I have no credibility in the "I'd never" department. I try not to make those kinds of pronouncements anymore because, more often than not, I end up doing them and am happier for it.

Acting in *Blades of Glory* definitely falls into that category. Mind you, I took a giant leap of faith. You never really know how a movie is going to turn out until it is edited. So much can change. A joke that seems palatable on paper can come off totally different on camera. But I threw caution to the wind and went for it. I liked that the movie grabbed the skating world around its neck and gave it a playful rub. It didn't ridicule skating; it just satirized it to perfection. And I felt it was good for the sport and good for me—considering all the morose seriousness of my life in recent times.

The risk was that the movie wouldn't play funny and the US

Figure Skating Association brass wouldn't be happy with it. Before the film came out in 2007, I went to the National Championships in Spokane, Washington, and told everyone who would listen how good the movie would be for skating. The film was still being edited, but I had seen pieces of it and could tell it would be a gem and would draw people to the sport of skating. Competitive skating had grown less glamorous and relevant in recent years, and I thought a satire of the more old-school silliness of competitive figure skating from a major movie studio would attract a new, younger audience. I remember telling the head of the skating association, "This is the best thing that could ever happen to skating." Sure enough, by the end of the tournament, some of the top committee members were sneaking up to their hotel suites, showing friends the trailer posted on the movie's Web site. The US Figure Skating Association couldn't endorse it officially, since it is still a very conservative body. But, internally, I have to give them credit for acknowledging that the sport could benefit from making fun of itself for two hours. And it really did.

THE SERIOUS RESULTS OF
TAKING LIFE SERIOUSLY

Maybe it was being born with literally the short end of the stick. Maybe it was losing my hair at a younger age. Maybe it was enduring the debilitating effects of cancer and a brain tumor. Maybe it's just the wisdom that can come from aging. Whatever the reason, I have learned that you just can't take anything too seriously. Most hypertension, heart attacks, breakups, lawsuits, and violent crimes result from people failing to step back, appreciate life, and realize whatever is bugging them just isn't that important. What matters is that we have been given life each day, that we have friends and family we love and who love us, that we have health and a happy outlook on life. These are the things that matter, not how much money you make or how jealous you are of the next guy or how your abs are better than your neighbor's.

> Whatever the reason, I have learned that you just can't take anything too seriously.

If you are the kind of person who takes yourself too seriously, then pray that you are never the subject of a parody sketch on *Saturday Night Live*.

I had the great fortune (or misfortune, if you want to look at it that way) of being parodied by not one, but two *SNL* comedians back in the 1990s. The first one was done by Dana Carvey, who, I have to say, really had my peppy, short-guy enthusiasm down. He did a mock skating commentary with the late comic genius Phil Hartman, playing Verne Lundquist, that was simply sidesplitting. From what I understand, Carvey really enjoyed playing me and, in fact, was once asked in an interview while promoting *Wayne's World* how the shooting was going, and he replied, "I don't know. I am trying to get down my Scott Hamilton imitation." I suppose I could have sulked at being mocked, but I was honored that I was so quirky and eccentric a character that even the super-talented Dana Carvey found it a challenge to imitate me!

But Carvey's impersonation was nothing compared to the one

David Spade once did of yours truly. Spade's Scott Hamilton was truly over-the-top. He wore this ridiculously ugly blonde wig that not only poofed skyward but revealed a very bald forehead. He didn't even have to say anything. The wig alone was a riot.

God didn't give us big ears, receding hairlines, spare tires, or oddly shaped feet not to laugh at them. And why would God give some of us giant bald heads that make us look like aliens if He didn't mean for it to be a joke? I mean, giant bald heads look funny. They just do. You have to laugh.

> True happiness doesn't come until you accept your flaws.

All of us have certain qualities or traits that we don't like about ourselves. We all have at one time or another looked in the mirror and said, "I wish that was better; I wish that looked different." Whether you're struggling with obesity or you're a super-model convinced that your nose doesn't photograph well from the left, everyone has something they perceive as a flaw.

True happiness doesn't come until you accept your flaws. You don't have to necessarily like them, but you must accept them as God-given and perfectly flawed. Once you do this, you can learn to laugh at them and make light of them.

I knew I had mastered the art of laughing at my flaws the day I met world-famous TV host and author Art Linkletter on an airport shuttle bus in Los Angeles several years ago. I introduced myself because I had grown up watching him on his CBS show *House Party*, in which he would ask kids adult questions and they'd give the cutest answers.

Linkletter, who is now in his mid 90s, replied, "I know who you are. You're the skater!"

I was so honored that *the* Art Linkletter, who I had always revered, knew who I was. Mr. Linkletter continued, "And you've been through so much. I mean, you've gone through a childhood illness, right? And you've battled cancer. It's so inspiring."

"Yeah, I sure did," I said, proud that he knew so much about my personal story.

And then, with no hint of sarcasm, he added, "And losing your hair publicly."

He was right; I did go bald *publicly*. But he said it as if going bald was an illness! Just when I was being showered with praise and ego-stroking from a childhood idol, he took me back down to earth by pointing out probably my second greatest physical characteristic (next to being short!). And it just made me laugh, the folly of it all.

I am a short, bald, chemo'd, brain-radiated, surgically repaired, *male* figure skater of unknown ethnic origin. What choice do I have but to be optimistic? It's almost more of a practical choice. I can either laugh or cry, and I decided a long time ago that crying just doesn't suit me.

COMIC RELIEF

I have found that people who have competed in sports on a high level tend to be able to make fun of themselves a little more easily than those uninitiated by the sports fraternity. I have been around hockey players who bust on each other more while sharing drinks after the game than they hit each other on the ice. It's part of the culture. Figure skaters can be no less jokingly brutal to one another. There can be so much pressure to be perfect that it's a relief when your peers razz you about things. It helps relieve some of the pressure.

Canadian Skating Champion Kurt Browning, who is also a good friend, was always a pleasure to have around the rink. Whenever things were getting too serious, I could always rely on Kurt for some comic relief.

Kurt, who was on tour with me for Stars on Ice, came to visit me in the hospital the day after I learned I had testicular cancer, and he brought me a "present." It was a little ball that looked like a testicle.

"Here you go," he said, handing it to me. "Just in case you need a spare."

Now, maybe you had to be there, but I thought that was really funny. It made me laugh so hard I cried. Now that's good crying! We also got a good laugh when he informed me of the name of the arena in Dayton, Ohio, where I would miss my first show due to the cancer. He made sure to tell me it was called the Nutter Center.

Another humorous aspect of being me is that a lot people assume that I am gay because I am a figure skater. It happens all the time, but one time stood out more than any other.

I was Christmas shopping with Tracie and our son, Aidan. We were at Macy's, and Aidan needed to go to the bathroom. Tracie took him in, and I waited outside in a chair that was part of the waiting room for the beauty shop.

An attractive older woman walked in wearing a Christmas sweater that I complimented her on. She recognized me and was very complimentary about my skating and career. I thanked her, and she took a seat about four chairs from mine.

Aidan came running out of the bathroom and jumped into my arms. The woman looked over and asked, "Is that your sister's son?" I said, "No, this is my son, Aidan."

She got very uncomfortable and said hesitantly, "Oh, uh . . . I never pictured you as the, uh, type to ever . . . start a family."

That was probably the nicest way anyone has ever tried to tell me, "I thought you were gay!"

A few years ago, I attended a Comedy Central roast of my good friend William Shatner. Bill has taught me a lot of what I know about not taking yourself too seriously. Bill is a good-natured, humble guy who is a pleasure to be around. And he was a good sport during what turned out to be the most brutal roast of an actor I had ever seen. For almost two hours, roaster after roaster poked fun at nearly everything about him. An onslaught came from Greg Giraldo, Andy Dick, Sandra Bullock, Farrah Fawcett, Jimmy Kimmel, Lisa Lampanelli, Betty White, and even his *Star Trek* costar Leonard "Dr. Spock" Nimoy. But Bill took it all in very good humor.

The comedians didn't limit their roasting to Bill. I was sitting near the stage with my friend and neighbor, Brad Paisley, who was wearing his signature cowboy hat. Well, one comedian kept calling Brad "Brokeback," insinuating that Brad was a less-than-macho cowboy. Poor Brad. It certainly didn't help that he was sitting next to a world-famous *male figure skater*. At one point, Brad turned to me and teased, "No offense, but sitting next to you is probably the last place I want to be right now!"

Veteran actress Betty White wasn't spared ridicule either. One of the comedians joked that Betty was so ancient the grand prize given on her first game show appearance was "fire." Betty genuinely laughed so hard it was contagious to us all.

But no one was more self-deprecating that night than Bill Shatner, who laughed at all the jokes along with the audience. Seeing Bill laugh at himself was inspiring. If Bill could howl with laughter while friends and comedians poked fun at his flaws, then I could certainly handle my own shortcomings with a sense of humor. I think finding humor in our shortcomings is something we could all do better.

GIVE YOUR POSITIVE MUSCLES A WORKOUT

Some bad things are going to happen, but more great things are going to happen. If you tend to see more bad than good, then you have to build that positive muscle in your brain much like an athlete does certain muscles to execute a certain move.

There's such beauty in this world. Yes, it can be hard to see it through all the negativity in the media and the dark outlook so many people seem to have. I turn on the news and see that as a society, we're struggling with letting the evil overshadow the good. We have to remind ourselves that the news industry is going to focus on tragedy and misery first. Good news isn't quite as marketable.

There are conflicts of interest and certain businesses that aren't being fair to their customers. People are losing their homes while

CEOs receive huge bonuses. But for every calamity and horrible thing happening in the world, there is something inspiring and beautiful happening too.

God gave us the gift of laughter as a tonic to fight all the desperation and despair in the world. Use that gift, and I guarantee that you'll find, whatever difficult things you are going through, you, like Kristi Yamaguchi, will be able to smile through them.

CHAPTER SIX

WIN BY GOING LAST

In skating, going last holds an advantage. Back when I competed, it was especially true. Scoring was based on the 6.0 points system, which meant that judges would withhold giving a skater early in the competition a perfect 6.0 in order to give remaining skaters a chance to win. I quickly learned that going last was always ideal.

Even today, with the scoring system now based on accumulated points earned by a skater's performance of various elements, there is an advantage to going last. If you go last, you know how many points you will need to win and can adjust your program accordingly. If the points show that landing a triple perfectly still won't give you a win, you know that you can go for a quad. You can pull off a win on difficulty of spins alone. By going later, after all the other skaters, you know what it will take to win and can use the system to your advantage.

In life, we need to remember that the same holds true. Yet our culture has become all about *me first.* Going last—whether it's being the last one on your block to have an SUV or the last one to sign up your kids for Little League—is viewed as a character flaw. Of course, not every culture is as obsessed with having to do everything first. In most American boardrooms, the CEO will speak first, will address his team first, and is expected to lead by being out in front of the pack. Whereas in Japan, often the most powerful person in the boardroom is the person who speaks the least and who speaks last. I bet we could learn a lot from this example of leadership.

THE REWARDS OF PUTTING OTHERS FIRST

Becoming a parent puts you on the fast track to the rewards of putting others first. Before Aidan was born, I had always considered myself a pretty caring, compassionate guy who took time out for others. I was involved in a lot of charities, trying to be generous with my time, whether helping young skaters or giving back to the skating community. I guess I considered myself a fairly selfless guy. But when I had kids, I soon realized how selfish I really was. My golf outings went from several times a week to maybe once every other month. Relaxing in front of the TV became the exception rather than the rule.

All that *free* time I had enjoyed before was now filled with putting Aidan down for naps, catching up on my own sleep, changing diapers, feedings, shopping—basically, being a domesticated dad. While fathering is a glorious and beautiful job, I would be lying if I didn't admit that sometimes I just wanted to get away and have some *me* time. It's a common reaction for a lot of new parents, and I was not immune to it.

Once I got through the initial "shock and awe" that the world no longer revolved around *moi*, I discovered that caring and sacrificing myself for this little creature made me a better, happier person. Being responsible for this tiny, helpless person's well-being and survival made all my selfish obsessions and problems seem petty and unimportant. By focusing so much energy on someone else, I spent less time worrying about things that, in the big picture, don't matter so much in the moment. Sure, I had to keep my career moving forward so that I could provide for my family, but I no longer spent several hours a day plotting, overanalyzing, and strategizing. I realized much of it was unnecessary.

> By focusing so much energy on someone else, I spent less time worrying about things that, in the big picture, don't matter so much in the moment.

On top of that, I found that I spent far less time worrying about my health and appearance. Should I take that speaking gig or not? Did I inject just the right amount of testosterone today? Does my hair need a buzz? Finding these answers became less urgent concerns. Instead, Aidan's health and well-being became my primary concern.

I would like to think that my parents raised me so well that I didn't need to have kids in order to become a more generous, selfless person, but I can't. I'm only human, after all.

SEEING THINGS FROM ANOTHER PERSPECTIVE

As I began putting myself in the backseat, I started to reassess everything in my life, all the choices I was making. I used to travel a lot, delivering speeches all around the country, with half my time spent on the road. After I became a father, I only wanted to travel if it was a must. Soon, the whole idea of living in Los Angeles began not to make sense either. Don't get me wrong. I love LA. The weather is perfect, I have many great, interesting friends there, and there is so much entertainment and recreation that you can never be bored. Plus, there are plenty of ice rinks with very skilled coaches. As a single guy, and even as a married guy without kids, Southern California is hard to beat.

> As I began putting myself in the backseat, I started to reassess everything in my life, all the choices I was making.

Yet for Tracie and me, the Southern California lifestyle began to make less sense—not so much for us, but for our growing family. Tracie had grown up in Jackson, Tennessee, and, of course, I was raised in Bowling Green, Ohio. We both felt that growing up in small towns, surrounded by family, away from the distractions and bustle of an urban center, instilled us with great values. We enjoyed the year-round tennis and golf, the endless sunny days, and all the fun of LA, but after talking and praying about it, we both concluded it was time for our family to leave California. Not so much for us, but for Aidan and the other children we hoped to have in the future.

Nashville made the most sense for us. My parents are deceased, and I no longer have family in Ohio, but Tracie's entire family remains in Tennessee. We wanted Aidan to have the same network of family love and support that we enjoyed as children, and Nashville was the perfect place to find that. We also went from having a tiny patch of grass for a backyard to living on more than four acres of land where our kids could play and the dogs could go crazy.

Plus, Nashville is geographically central in the United States. I could still hop on a flight to LA or New York with relative ease. So in May 2006, we sold our house, packed up everything, and moved to Nashville.

Even though we sometimes miss our friends or some of the professional opportunities in LA, we are so much happier for moving. The reason can be seen on the faces of our sons, Aidan and Maxx, when they get to see their grandparents, aunts, uncles, and cousins as much as they do, and when I get to spend the kind of quality time with them that LA makes difficult due to traffic, hectic schedules, and all the distractions of big-city life.

Recently, it was a gorgeous spring day in Nashville, and I told Aidan we could do whatever he wanted for the afternoon. He said he wanted to go for a bike ride. So we went out and did that for a while until, as five-year-olds are apt to do, he got bored. Then we rode scooters. But when we got back to the garage, I noticed his red Radio Flyer wagon sitting in the corner, covered in spider webs and dust, untouched since our arrival in Nashville. We had bought the wagon when we lived in LA but rarely ever used it, because there was a lot of traffic around our home and there wasn't a convenient, safe place for him to ride it.

So I go, "Aidan, do you want to clean up your wagon?" I knew this was going to be a hit. *Something new!*

Predictably, he said, "Yeah!"

We got out all the car wash stuff—buckets, soap, sponges, towels. Aidan filled up his toy spray gun with water and started spraying down the wagon while I hosed it off. We filled up buckets, made the suds, and scrubbed down the wagon. Then I accidentally sprayed him with the hose, and he shot me this mischievous look and splashed me back. I sprayed him back and, suddenly, we were having a huge water fight in our driveway. All Aidan wanted to do was get wet and get me wet. So I would give him the hose, and he would try to squirt me before I grabbed it back and chased him down. We were both drenched. And he was laughing so hard with an expression of absolute joy. It was so much fun.

Eventually, he got exhausted and cold, so I wrapped him in a blanket and let him relax the rest of the day. Around that time, I had begun having some doubts about whether the move from LA had been entirely the right one for me. Away from managers and agents and my friends in the entertainment industry, I had been feeling a little out of the loop professionally. And I was right. I was out of the loop, and it wasn't the best thing for me as a performer.

But that day with Aidan was all I needed to convince me that we had made the right decision to move to Tennessee. Seeing the pure joy on his face of getting into a water fight with his dad was priceless. And you know what? So was the look on mine, I'd imagine. By putting my family first and my own needs second, I was in fact winning the game of life. I had put myself into a new loop that made me happier and more fulfilled. And it has made me a better husband and father.

LEARNING FROM POSITIVE
EXAMPLES OF OTHERS

As a skater, I have long known the advantage of watching others make mistakes before you. But even before all my skating success, my mom taught me by example the virtue of letting others go before you.

My mother was selfless. She put her family first, behind her own needs. She led by going last. She would do without so that we could have. My mother would never buy new clothes for herself. She always felt that the money spent on her was better spent on her kids or saved. She was a true leader.

But my mom truly inspired me in a way that no one ever has. In fact, it was the season after her death that my skating career took off. Why? Because I wanted to do it for her so badly that I worked harder than ever. She had sacrificed so much to get me to a place where I could be a world-class skater, and because she had put me first all her life, I was determined to give everything I had to honor her. She never got to see me win Nationals or Worlds or a Gold

Medal at the Olympics, and to this day, I regret that more than anything.

Mother gave up nearly everything to keep me in skating, yet she never got to enjoy my highest achievements. She certainly enjoyed her children, but she never really got to feel special and be pampered. I always sensed that she struggled with self-esteem, yet she was so brave in her battle with cancer, and she was so amazing for the students she counseled while she was obtaining her associate professorship at Bowling Green State University. If she were alive today, after giving her the biggest hug and kissing her a thousand times and telling her how much I love her, I would take her shopping in the nicest mall and buy her anything she wanted because she never had the money to splurge on herself.

> I was blessed to have a mother and father who were so loving and unselfish.

She faced the challenge of my illnesses and of keeping me in skating. All those things really took its toll on her. And after all that personal sacrifice, she died of cancer. I have always felt that I had to honor her sacrifices and her suffering. And I did that by trying to work as hard as I could in skating.

When I look back, up until the point of her death—except for the US Junior Championship—I underachieved consistently. It wasn't until after she died that I really took on the challenge and did well as an amateur competitor and later professionally. From that time forward, my ability to train and compete and be what she thought I could be continued to improve.

I was blessed to have a mother and father who were so loving and unselfish. And, amazingly, I also had the great fortune of having another set of parental figures in my life who also taught me the rewards of putting other people before yourself.

LIVES WORTH WATCHING

Frank and Helen McLoraine, an older couple from Chicago, were my financial sponsors throughout my teen years and into my twenties. Carlo Fassi connected us in 1976. They were so very generous to me. They funded my skating so I could have the chance to compete at a world-class level. My parents had taken me as high as they could, but they were going broke doing it. Frank and Helen were like angels, and they also became like parents to me.

After my mother died, I went to spend some time with Frank and Helen at their house. Frank said, "You know, Helen and I would love to help fill the void left by the loss of your mother as best we can. We'd like to be in your life in that way." I was so touched that he would say that, especially since I had only known them for a little over a year at that point. "We're here for you in every capacity," he said. And they were!

Frank and Helen understood everything I'd been through and wanted to support me no matter what. Frank died from a rare blood disease in May 1979, and it was devastating to lose him two years after losing my mom. But because he was so giving, I learned so much from this man in such a short period of time.

Frank was one of the most charming, wonderful, giving people

I'd ever met in my life. He and Helen were partners. Frank was a wealthy family and estate attorney and practiced law in downtown Chicago. His offices were in the giant Temple Building across from the Daley Center. He was wise and well spoken, tall and handsome, and his personality was very charismatic. I learned so much from him just by spending time around him. He always told the same jokes, which I loved. Things like, when we'd go to a restaurant, he'd ask the maitre d' for a table "overlooking the bill." And he had no problem with laughing at his own corny jokes. He had such a great sense of humor that you always wanted to be in his company.

Helen, on the other hand, was more reserved in public. But she was fiercely intelligent. While Frank took the social lead, Helen did a lot of the heavy lifting when it came to business decisions because she was so sharp. They were a great team and traveled everywhere together. They had gotten into the business of sponsoring skaters because they both loved the sport and wanted to help other people live their dreams. It was that pure for them. They didn't want anybody to ever have to give up on something because of a lack of money when they had more than enough.

Helen's whole philosophy was to give. She and Frank didn't have their own children, so they focused their love and attention on skaters and other philanthropic efforts. Throughout Helen's life, she gave away half of everything she and Frank made to charity every year, and the rest of it accumulated to where it was given to charity on her passing.

When she and Frank were together, you could see that she

always had a sparkle in her eye because he was so charming and fun to be around, and everybody loved him. Frank often said that life would feel empty if he didn't give back and share it with others.

One example of Frank giving back to others is the way he took care of an elderly gentleman who had helped him when he was younger. When I would be in a show or a competition in Chicago, he would usually come, along with this elderly gentleman. Frank would take his elderly friend everywhere: to my competitions, to my exhibitions, to dinners. It was touching to see how much Frank cared for his friend. He was always so thoughtful, and it set such a good example for me. He was dedicated to creating an atmosphere of comfort and levity around him, and there was, more often than not, a little bit of a lesson in everything that he said.

One time when I was visiting Frank and Helen, I got a speeding ticket near their house. Frank was very connected politically in his neighborhood; he knew all the people in the police department and the legal profession. I was at the age when I had all the excuses. "I'm sure I wasn't speeding," I protested. "It wasn't my fault."

Frank listened to my immature excuse and just shook his head. He said, "Okay. I'll take care of this. Don't worry about it." Frank went to the traffic court judge and managed to get me off. Afterward, he called me and said, "I got you out of the ticket by pleading *non compos mentis.*"

Being totally naive of legal mumbo jumbo, I asked, "What's that?"

"It means that you're mentally incapable of standing trial," he said, laughing.

Frank's lesson was clear: *I love you. I got you off, but don't be stupid.*

Many times I saw people being rude or dishonest to Frank, but he never took the bait and went to their level. He also showed me how important it was to keep things simple.

We once went to a very fancy restaurant in Colorado Springs at the Broadmoor hotel. It was the kind of place where well-dressed servers are coming up to your table constantly. Though wealthy, Frank wasn't comfortable with such fuss and formality. We ordered our dishes and then got into a deep, private conversation. Since some of the food had to be prepared at the table, every minute someone on the staff would come by and have to touch the food, check and make sure we were okay. Well, it started to annoy him after a while because we were trying to have a conversation and enjoy our dinner, but the wait staff kept interrupting by messing with the dinner. So after about a dozen interruptions, the maitre d' came back and started stirring and fussing with the food. Frank asked, "Does everybody get to touch this piece of food?" And the maitre d' replied, "Well, we just want it to be perfect." He looked at me and said, "I told you we should have gone to Wendy's."

> Although he has been gone for thirty years, Frank's legacy is alive and well—especially in the pages of this book.

Frank also impressed upon me how important it is to be truthful. If he ever sensed I wasn't being entirely honest, he would say with a little sparkle in his blue eyes, "You know, if you never lie, you'll never have to remember what you said."

To this day, I find myself saying things Frank would say. Although he has been gone for thirty years, Frank's legacy is alive and well—especially in the pages of this book. In fact, if I thought the publisher would let me, I could easily title this book, *What Would Frank Do?*

Frank and Helen possessed a secret to being happy that too few people grasp. They knew that giving—passing on wisdom, donating to charity, funding skaters, helping the elderly—was a key to finding happiness. But they didn't teach me this valuable lesson by simply telling me; they did it through example, which is a far more powerful way to send a message.

WINNING AS A "NUMBER TWO"

Another man who was responsible for shaping my positive attitude was a European-born show skater named Fritz Dietl. He was a rink owner, skating coach, inventor, entrepreneur, and former star of Sonia Henie's ice shows. But, mostly, he was a very smart man who gave so much to those around him.

I was in a pro competition in South Africa and was having a great time after the event was over. Fritz pulled me aside to give me a life lesson that would change my perspective forever.

He said, "Do you want a long career?"

"Of course," I said.

"Then always be a number two," he said. "Always put someone above you. Never put yourself first."

Now this is a man who performed with the greatest diva in the history of pro skating. Sonia Henie was a huge star and always put herself first and made a fortune doing just that. But here was a man telling me to put others first.

Seeing that I was captured by his advice, he continued, "Number ones come and go, but a number two can last forever."

> "Number ones come and go, but a number two can last forever."

It was an amazing nugget of wisdom. There is an Olympics every four years with new stars and new excitement. How am I going to survive that in a long career? I decided that he was probably right and started my long journey as a self-proclaimed "number two."

I applied this mentality in the early days of Stars on Ice. I knew that building this company was going to take time, and I was in it for the long haul. How was I going to convince skaters to tour with me when they had their own brands to build? The answer was to make sure that they knew they were going to be presented as a star. Not a costar.

When we were on our first five-city tour as a prototype show, even though I was the spokesperson for the show, I made sure that all the skaters had their star moments. I worked feverishly to make sure the show was as good as it could be without being burdened with the image as the be-all and end-all.

The show went together smoothly, but the tour was a bumpy ride technically. We didn't really know how to do it. As we traveled to various cities, we were without a local crew, and our road crew was getting burned out. Our permanent traveling road crew consisted of five guys living in a Winnebago and going from small town to small town setting up the show with no help. No local crew meant that these guys had to work harder and start earlier after driving all night to get to the next city. We were coming into Morristown, New Jersey, and I got the news that for the fourth day in a row we had no local crew at the building for the load-in. Our guys had hit the wall and couldn't take another step forward.

I was at the Newark Airport when I heard the bad news and jumped into a cab with our lighting director Paul Thibert. We arrived at the rink, and our crew was apologetic, saying that we would have to do the show without lights and they were really sorry that they had nothing left in the tank to make another show happen without a crew.

I said that I understood but that I would be happy to throw on some gloves and help unload the trucks. That sent a message to them that this was more than a gig to me. I was exhausted too. We just had done all these shows in a row with no time off to catch up on rest, getting up at 5 a.m. every day to get to the next small city for the next performance.

They thought, *If he is willing to help, we can do this.* And they did it. That show was a huge one. Torvill and Dean, along with many other skaters, came in from New York City to see this new start-up company. So did Dick Button and many executives from ABC Sports, including Doug Wilson and Dennis Lewin. The show went great, and our reputation started to grow.

Another way of leading by putting myself last was to let every star of the show know that this was their vehicle to build a long career. At first, I'm sure that Brian Orser wasn't sure about being in "my" show. But I convinced him that this was an opportunity for him to come in and make this opportunity *his* and then take it to Canada after the US tour.

This philosophy was genuine and worked for everyone who came into our Stars on Ice family. Debi Thomas came in as our *new* star. So did Peter and Kitty Carruthers, Gordeeva and Grinkov, Tracy Wilson and Rob McCall, Torvill and Dean, Katarina Witt, Kurt Browning, Paul Wylie, Tara Lipinski, Ilia Kulik, Sale and Pelletier, Alexei Yagudin, and many, many more.

> My favorite contribution to the tour was done behind the scenes, communicating our needs to the powers-that-be without making anyone feel like I was the boss.

There were so many great stars, but I don't think anyone exemplified the impact of the new star quite like Kristi Yamaguchi. She led purely by example. No one worked harder and skated more consistently. I would happily and gratefully be a "number two" to her for the rest of my career.

I do think, however, that my favorite contribution to the tour was done behind the scenes, communicating our needs to the powers-that-be without making anyone feel like I was the boss. I would skate hard every night for the audience, make sure the skaters were happy, make sure the crew knew they were appreciated, and keep the marquee strong by presenting new champion talent as the new "number ones."

How long would the tour last if my name was on it above the title? Probably not very long. Stars on Ice fans love to be acquainted with the skaters they are going to see, but longevity depends on a fresh product and new stars and ideas. That's why Stars on Ice has been so successful, I believe—we continually add skaters to the tour and feature new "number one" stars.

And my inspiration for running the show in this unselfish way was the sage advice from Fritz Dietl.

LEARNING FROM OTHERS' MISTAKES

I learned so much from people in my life who went out of their way to show me, teach me, and sacrifice for me. But I also learned a lot from people who had no idea that they were teaching me: those I watched make mistakes.

A big part of my success in skating was seeing what other people did well then trying to do that. But I also learned from seeing how people would completely mess themselves up, and then I would try not to do that. There are a couple of ways to learn that a stove is hot. You can touch it and burn your finger, or you can see that someone else who touched it burned himself. I prefer learning from the latter. But I see so many times in life when people insist on making the mistake themselves and get burned. I don't know if it is ego or pride or what it is, but it's just not necessary. Has anyone ever seen a happy criminal in jail? No. But that doesn't stop people from stealing every day. I would see skaters try jumps they had no business attempting. Either they didn't have the skill level, or the ice surface was bad and made the jump dangerous, but even if others before them tried and failed, they would go for it anyway and bite it. So going last only holds an advantage if you use it as an opportunity to learn from others. If you don't, then the only thing going last gets you is home later than everyone else.

There's no question that putting others first is a recipe for success in many things in life. Take the example of the workplace. Perhaps you want to be the supervisor, the top manager. All too often, people mistakenly think that putting down others is the way to get ahead. But the opposite is true. Start by giving compliments to your staff, being considerate. Stand them up, build up their shoulder strength, and on their shoulders they will carry you to your destination.

You can try this out in everyday life. Tell your wife she looks beautiful today. Compliment your friends on their achievements. Write thank-you notes to people who have helped you. Call your grandmother and tell her how much she means to you. Focus on building up others, and your own sense of self-worth will improve. Some call these random acts of human kindness. But the truth is, acting unselfishly is not random at all. Instead, it is a conscious, concerted effort to make the world better by making someone else's life better. The bonus: you will be happier by doing it.

CHAPTER SEVEN

Learn a New Routine

The only thing constant about this life is that changes will happen every day. How we handle these changes is entirely up to us. As I mentioned earlier, my friend Eric Heiden liked to point out that it's not the changes in our lives that define us; it's our response to those changes that will define us and, ultimately, determine our level of happiness.

Whether we like it or not, nothing will be the same tomorrow as it is today. In fact, scientists tell us that things change from one nanosecond to the next. Cells die and are reborn. Hair constantly falls out, and new hair grows in (except, of course, in my case). The atmosphere changes with each emission of gas, every drop of rain.

The earth's rotation changes ever so slightly with each turn. Human life is defined by change. Your job will change. Your boss will change. Your spouse may change. Your needs will change. Your body will change. Learning not to fight the inevitable changes life brings is a key component to being happy.

> Learning not to fight the inevitable changes life brings is a key component to being happy.

With change comes unpredictability, uncertainty, and the unknown. That, more than anything else, can make people so anxious that they will avoid having to accept change.

CHANGE IS PART OF GOD'S PLAN

I had to learn from an early age that change was an inevitable part of God's plan. As a kid, I was in and out of hospitals—feeling well one day, and feeling like I had one foot in the grave the next. My very mortality was an ever-changing adventure of highs and lows that were seemingly out of my control. My body was always in a state of change. Many nights, I would lie in a hospital alone overnight, wondering what the doctors were going to do to me the next morning. Would it be more painful, scary stuff, or would the doctors finally have an answer for me? Either way, it would mean more change.

Having no self-esteem because of my illnesses, I arrived at the Bowling Green State University Ice Arena at age nine for my first skating lesson with a feeding tube in my nose and barely any muscular development.

That first day of clinging to the wall was difficult, and I fell more times than I can count. It was uncomfortable, a risk to my fragile health, a change from the daily comfort of being cared for by my mother. But it was a change that also marked the first day of a change-filled journey that would eventually lead to winning an Olympic Gold Medal. I would go to the rink once a week, which led to three times a week and private lessons, which, by the time I was in high school, had evolved into me moving away from home to train as a skater (talk about a change!) because that was the best for my skating future. Then there was the traveling, the compulsory figure tests, the training and learning new jumps and techniques every day. Coaching changes, moving to new living situations in different cities—nothing was the same year to year. Success meant being able to change for the better every day. That took me to higher levels of success, which eventually helped me become who I am today. The whole process, by definition, meant one change after another.

> We often fight things that are uncomfortable.

Still, we often fight things that are uncomfortable. We resist what may take us to a better place.

EMBRACE THE CHANGE

Even at times when I knew I needed to change personally in my life, I would resist it. I remember being in Ottawa for the Canadian tour of Stars on Ice. The catered meal that day was in a room next to the physical therapy room in the new arena and the walls were covered with inspirational messages. There had to be dozens of positive, uplifting messages meant to inspire the NHL's Ottawa Senators to greater heights. I looked around this room and was amazed by all the inspirational quotes. The one that stuck most in my mind and hit me the hardest was the old nautical saying: "No journey truly begins until you can no longer see dry land."

In other words, don't put one foot on shore and one in the boat and think you're going somewhere. It's not going to work. You've got to push away from the shore and be prepared for what may or may not be a bumpy ride. And then, once you're not that change-fearing person anymore, you can truly embrace your metamorphosis.

> I'm a big believer that change is just another word for opportunity.

Risk and change go hand in hand. I haven't had anything happen in my life that didn't begin with taking some risk. But I'm a big believer that *change* is just another word for opportunity. Change is a test of our strength that, if we pass, gives us the opportunity to move on and be more productive, more satisfied and happier. Because I have experienced so many great things after embracing change in my life—going from amateur to pro, skater to commentator, young to middle-aged, single to married with kids—I have learned to love the passages from one stage to the next. And you can too.

To resist change is futile. Unfortunately, our culture increasingly encourages people to combat natural life changes, especially when it comes to aging. Wrinkles? Get a facelift! Spare tire? Get liposuction!

Going bald? Get a hair weave. There are some physical changes that are just a fact of life, and for me going bald is one of them. When I started losing my hair in my twenties, I had a choice. I could have gotten a hair weave or a toupee. I could have let vanity get the best of me and fought my body's transition. But I didn't. It just never made sense to me. Now I would be lying if I didn't admit that I tried a few things to disguise my receding hairline. Yet after my chemo, I decided that I didn't care anymore that I was losing my hair. God gave me this beautiful bare head for a reason. Why? I don't know, but I don't need to know. I just have to accept and love myself for who I am and embrace it. So far, so good.

CHANGE CAN BE A STRUGGLE

We all know that change can be a struggle. When things are going well, we don't want anything to change; we prefer the status quo. But when things aren't working out, we desperately want change. The brutal truth is that we can't have it both ways. We have to take the good with the bad and accept that even the good stuff will have its cycle played out.

I learned this when I came back from the 1984 Olympics. During that time, I was a resident of Colorado, living and training in Denver. So when I came back, I was something of a hometown hero in Colorado.

A local businessman, Bill Daniels, was taken by the story *Sports Illustrated* did on me as a preview of the Olympics. After I won my Gold Medal, he sent his jet to bring me back to Denver where there would be a giant celebration. The town rolled out the red carpet for me with marching bands, a fire truck filled with cheerleaders, and a full parade to take me to historic Larimer Square from the airport for a ceremony that included the mayor of Denver, the governor's wife, my favorite jazz band, and testimonials from civic leaders. There were about five thousand people there to celebrate, and I was overwhelmed by the level of support I was given by my hometown. After the parade and ceremony, it was on to the local comedy nightclub for a show and a never-ending presentation of gifts from merchants from all over the state of Colorado.

The attention was a bit overwhelming. You have to understand. I had won the Gold Medal far away in the mountains of Yugoslavia, and while there were a lot of American fans and media at the games, I didn't get a real sense of how much—or if—people back home cared about my victory.

I connected through Chicago's O'Hare airport on my way back to Denver, and I remember going down to the baggage claim, just as I had so many times before. In fact, I had gone through O'Hare on my way to Sarajevo just weeks earlier and had been in the same terminal, asking people for the time because I didn't have a watch on me, but no one paid any attention to me. I had to ask almost ten people for the time before one of them actually stopped to literally give me the time of day!

On the way home, however, I was standing at the baggage claim, and someone recognized me and asked for an autograph. Then another person noticed and then another, and the next thing I knew, I spent the next hour taking photos with fans and signing autographs.

Back in Denver, the city held a huge parade for me. Thousands showed up for a ticker tape parade through downtown streets. It was humbling, amazing, and downright shocking. The country had never before embraced a male figure skater as they had me. I was on cloud nine!

One of the calls I got when I came back was from the office of longtime Colorado governor Dick Lamm, who invited me up to his office at the state capitol. I got all dressed up, thinking it was going to be one of those photo ops where an aide tells the governor a few minutes beforehand, "Oh, we have that skater guy coming in for a quick photo." Politicians, especially ones who make it to high offices like governor, aren't known for their subtlety or lack of wanting media attention, after all. I assumed there would be a horde of press, photographers, and aides waiting for me the second I arrived.

Not that I didn't respect Lamm. He was an interesting guy. I had read that he worked as a lumberjack in Oregon and worked as a deckhand on an ore boat, in addition to having a law degree and serving as a first lieutenant in the army. Lamm was a reformer, the kind of guy who thought outside the box. In fact, one of his moves as governor, an office he held from 1975 to 1987, was to name folk singer John Denver the state's poet laureate. He was a neat guy. Still, he was a politician, so I expected he only wanted to meet me for publicity's sake.

I walked into Governor Lamm's office, and he was sitting there with another gentleman. I shook hands with them, and then the governor asked the other guy to leave. There we were, just the two of us alone! Lamm proceeded to tell me the reason he invited me to his office.

He said that after his wife, Dottie, had attended the parade, she really admired what I had accomplished. "I just wanted to talk to you," he said. I thought, *Just talk? No photos, no media coverage?* I was taken aback.

After congratulating me and asking me how I liked living in Colorado, he said, "You know, there's a thing called the 'hometown hero syndrome,' and I just want you to be aware of it."

"Uh-uh," I replied, even though I had no idea where he was going with this.

"I just want you to put this in your mind and please do not forget this," he continued. "Imagine you're the quarterback of the high school football team, and you throw the bomb at the end of the game to win the state championship. That's an incredible thing! Everyone loves you, you're the top dog, and all the girls want to hang out with you. Your family is so proud of you, and everyone in your world knows who you are. But that moment goes away, and it can be hard to deal with. If you don't realize this, you can suffer from hometown hero syndrome. After the moment goes away, it's then about who you are. What are you *really* about? What's next? You've got to put everything that's happened to you in its place and understand that, at least, when it comes to skating, this is probably as good as it gets, right now."

At first, I couldn't believe he just wanted to talk. Then I couldn't believe he wanted to rain on my parade! But, in truth, I was touched that he generously took the time out to counsel me about how to handle my success, how to prepare for the inevitable march of time that would lead me to not be such hot stuff anymore. I was so lucky that he passed on this wisdom to me right when I got back because his words ultimately proved correct, and I was better prepared for it. There soon would be another Olympics and another Olympic hero. He closed by telling me, "Enjoy it, soak it all in. You deserve it. But I just want you to keep in the back of your mind, as you embrace and enjoy all these moments, that this will not be going on the rest of your life."

People use the expression "This too shall pass" with good reason. The pendulum swings both ways—for good and bad. No question about it.

Things will change for all the people who suffered in high school at the hands of the popular kids. Whether you were the big jock or the big nerd, chances are that you are not going to be that person for the rest of your life. I have heard so many stories about people in high school and junior high and grade school who were mean to me, who bullied me. Many of those people ended up with not-so-great outcomes. For most people who were cruel in high school, that was as good as they ever had it in life. I point this out not to revel in their demise, but rather to make the point that things will change.

I've seen other skaters suffer from Dick Lamm's so-called hometown hero syndrome far too many times. I've seen people win an Olympic Gold Medal and think it's going to guarantee them a good living for the rest of their lives, that all they need to do is ride the wave of that success, and they are set. But it doesn't work out that way. Any Olympic success opens a door of opportunity that you have to find a way to kick in. You have to work hard to take advantage of the opportunity and leverage it to move on to the next level, the next challenge.

You've got to keep looking ahead. You can't get stuck in what you've already done. If you don't plan for tomorrow, then you won't know what to do when you get there. Steven Cousins once told me, "The questions of winter are answered in the summer." What he meant was that if you want to win a championship in the winter, you have to plant the seeds in the summer.

A Constant State of Change

The wheel of change is indeed constantly turning. It's been said, if you want to make God laugh, then just make a plan. No doubt, the plan will change! It's funny how I once thought by the time I was in my forties, things would slow down, that change wouldn't happen so much. Boy, was I wrong!

Tracie and I got engaged, married, and pregnant in the span of three months. I didn't have time for a midlife crisis because I was so busy living life! Talk about change. Those are three major life changes, all happening in a short period of time.

Also, my home life has been nothing but change over the past several years. My parents lived in the same town their entire professional lives, but I have lived in three different homes in just the first five years of marriage. When Tracie and I married, I lived in a lake house that made no sense for children. So after we had Aidan, we moved down the street to a more traditional-style home. It was a nice, two-story house on a golf course just north of LA. Then, about three years later, we packed up and moved to Nashville, where we bought a house thinking it would be where we raised our kids until they moved away to college. We really thought, *This is it. Let's settle in.* I actually remember saying, "That's it. I'm never moving again!" Well, two years into living in our Nashville home, we realized it was too big. We especially didn't like having the kids' bedrooms on a different

> You've got to keep looking ahead. You can't get stuck in what you've already done.

floor than ours. So we began plans to build a smaller home. Our family has changed, our needs changed, our wants are different than they were before.

And since Tracie and I married, our lives have been in a constant state of change. Thankfully, I am married to someone who views change the same way I do.

A Changing Perspective

We are always in the season of change, and with each change of season comes a new level of awareness and maturity and perspective. I think that's something that I've always understood. It has allowed me to keep my heart and mind open and embrace what comes next.

When my amateur career ended in 1984 and I turned pro, it was a major upheaval in my life. At the time, I was basically broke.

I was living in the basement apartment of a friend's house, and this wonderful family took care of me. Henry and Helen Landis were the parents I missed having in my life for a long time. They housed me because I was a friend of their son, Brent. Even though I was supposed to stay for just a couple of weeks until I found a permanent place to live, I ended up living there for three-and-a-half years.

After going pro, I was able to afford a condo, buy myself a car, and join the Ice Capades, making really good money for the first time in my life. Although it was a very egocentric world in many ways, it was also very humbling. Being a pro meant I was no longer in business just for myself; instead, I had to report to someone and had an entire staff relying on me. Sure, I had someone to sharpen my skates, pick out my clothes, select my music, and prepare the details for me so I could just show up and skate, but the flip side was I suddenly had a lot of responsibility to an entire production company. Before that, I was a production company with one employee: me. I had to grow up fast.

I was traveling to a different city every week, doing eight to twelve shows each week, along with publicity. As the headliner, it was my job to talk people into buying tickets for the show. I no longer had to perform in front of a panel of nine judges from nine different countries, but my new stress was convincing people to pay to come watch me. Depending on how good of a salesman I was, that could mean attracting twelve people or twelve thousand people. And, of course change being the rule, after two years of doing this for Ice Capades, the organization was going through change by being sold to a new owner with new ideas, and they eventually let me go. It was yet another round of change.

I recently appeared on *The Today Show* for a segment on "Turning 50." Host Matt Lauer was about to turn the big five-O, and since I was forty-nine I was invited to be part of a celebrity roundtable discussion that included comedian Bob Saget and Mark Cuban, the owner of the Dallas Mavericks.

It was kind of surreal being on the show to talk about turning fifty. I had been on *Today* many times over the years, and it seemed like only yesterday that I was on there, skating in Rockefeller Plaza after my 1984 Olympic win.

The conversation turned to the dreaded "midlife crisis," and it made me realize something: I never had one! At least, not a traditional one by any means.

> Cancer didn't allow me the self-destructive self-indulgence of a midlife crisis. Instead, it focused me on what was important, and I made positive changes.

"Well, you know, everybody talks about the midlife crisis, but I had an anti-midlife crisis," I said. "I turned forty and the first thing I did was get married, start a family, and become a Christian. I kind of went in the other direction."

It occurred to me that cancer didn't allow me the self-destructive self-indulgence of a midlife crisis. Instead, it focused me on what was important, and I made positive changes. Most important, perhaps, was that I didn't try to cheat time, as so many of us do in our forties and fifties.

Sure, it is jarring to age. You're living your life, you're going along, and then all of a sudden you count the candles on the cake and there are *fifty*. You can't help but think, *Wow, that was fast!* You regret not making the necessary life-changing decisions that help make you a more fulfilled and happy person. Too many times, people live life as a dress rehearsal, telling themselves, "I'll get to that someday." Well, you have only so many minutes on this planet, and if you spend them putting off making changes, then you are just wasting time. The last thing I want to say on my deathbed is, "I really wanted to do that, but time just got away from me."

FIGHTING FOR CHANGE

What I'm prescribing, and what I have tried to live, is fighting *for* change, not fighting against it.

Your body's changing. What I could do on the ice in 1984, I can't do anymore. You get older, you collect injuries, you collect experiences that either put you in a higher place artistically or a lower place athletically, and you're constantly dealing with that every single day. If you fight the aging process, it can get you down and make you not want to lace up your skates. But if you pay attention to it and enjoy the evolution, it can really enhance your life.

> What I'm prescribing, and what I have tried to live, is fighting for change, not fighting against it.

Many people absolutely hate change and do everything they can to resist it. They just want things to stay the same, in their comfort zone. But I don't want to be in high school again! I might look back and think those were wonderful years, which they were, but when I see those guys still wearing a mullet and listening to the same bands, I just cringe—about the mullet, that is. I think no matter what your high school experience was, you will always like listening to the music that was popular during that time. But as far as the "style of the day," I think every guy should live by the rule that if you are over thirty and still have a ponytail, get out the scissors. You have to move on.

Let it go.

You have to let go of one age to enjoy the next one. You have to accept where you are and learn a new routine. Every stage of life has something different to offer. In adolescence, it is all about being cool. Then in your twenties, you want to be taken seriously. In your thirties, you want to enjoy the ride a little . . . and it goes on and on. But you've got to let go of your twenties to enjoy your thirties, to let go of your thirties to be satisfied in your forties . . . and so on and so on. I am now looking forward to experiencing my fifties because I have never been there before. If you think of life as an amazing journey to places you have never been, suddenly it starts looking like an adventure.

Instead, a lot of us want to fight aging with plastic surgery and hair dye. I'm so tired of hearing commercials saying, "Tired of being bald? Don't you want that long, luxurious hair that all women love?" Give me a break! They try to make you cheat time, and doing so is just making a deal with the devil. Life is beautiful and perfect.

It was designed absolutely the way it should be, even the apparent imperfections. Embrace it all and you will be happy; fight it and you will exhaust yourself and lose a different battle.

Perhaps athletes learn this lesson quicker than most people since our livelihood is tied to our physical abilities, which undeniably dwindle with age. I knew that when I turned pro, I would need to change my presentation, my image, my, well, just about everything. I wanted to turn heads. I needed to learn a new routine. Millions had seen me perform my Olympic programs, and if they came out and saw me repeat those same moves—albeit with the stakes not as high—it would be a letdown for them. I didn't want to just go out there with the Gold Medal dangling around my neck and wave to the crowd like a beauty pageant winner. That's when I taught myself how to do the back flip.

Part of the appeal of the back flip to me was that back flips are illegal in amateur competitive skating. So I knew that if I could do back flips, it would be a bold statement that would turn some heads. Everyone would want to see my new trick. The back flip was part of an overhaul I undertook after turning pro. Even as an amateur, I tried to set myself apart visually. At a time when male figure skaters were wearing sparkling Spandex suits, I wore a speed skating suit instead. I didn't want it to be a costume party, but more of an athletic event. Not to mention it set me apart by making me look sleeker than I actually was.

As a pro, I became less of an athlete and more of an entertainer. My performances were more about wearing costumes and playing characters. I had to change and evolve as a skater, and learning the back flip would put an exclamation point on this wholesale change.

Many people think I was the first skater to do a back flip. Far from it! The back flip was a staple in ice shows for decades, with comedic ice show skaters doing it with great skill. I had seen it done many times but never had the time or the guts to learn it. First of all, it is a very dangerous jump. If one of my coaches had ever seen me even trying to do a back flip, I would have been in *big* trouble. They would have been the ones to flip!

At its heart, the back flip is as much a gymnastics move as it is a skating one. So when I set out to learn it, I enlisted the help of Greg Weiss, gymnastics coach and father of US National Champion Michael Weiss. Greg taught me first how to back flip on the padded floor. He would tie a towel around my waist and spot me as I attempted the jump. I took to it pretty quickly. The biggest obstacle—fear—was not much of a problem for me, which helped. But to take it out onto the ice too soon would have been suicide. One failed rotation, and I could crack my head open. It's dangerous because when you're going over and your toe slips, it's like pole vaulting and the pole slips out of the hole—you're going to crash in a bad way. So the key is that you have to make sure your toe sticks hard so you can throw yourself up in the air high enough. In fact, the last time I did the back flip was the day after I was diagnosed

> If one of my coaches had ever seen me even trying to do a back flip, I would have been in big trouble. They would have been the ones to flip!

with a brain tumor. It didn't go well. My toe didn't stick on the push off properly, and I only got up about halfway in the air and landed on my head, shoulder, and knee—in that order. I haven't tried it since.

Needless to say, I had to make sure I had the flip down off the ice before bringing it to the ice, where the physical stakes were much higher. I would practice flipping into a swimming pool and into a gymnastics landing pit. Eventually, I could do it without a spotter.

About six months into the process, I was eager to take the back flip onto the ice. A comedic skater by the name of Joey Percely, who had come from a long line of Percellis who did comedic ice routines, agreed to teach me the move. Joey was a natural gymnast, something I was not. What I learned is that the hardest part of doing a back flip on ice was landing it. I fell a few times and hurt my shoulder. So I would leave it alone for a few weeks and come back to it. If I was going to do a back flip, I couldn't have any fear. And Joey helped push me over the hump and get the technique down from beginning to end, helping me build the muscle memory.

Then, about a year after I had begun the learning process, I was ready to take it into a live show, which I did with great success. And I continued to do it nearly every show for the next fifteen years. It became my trademark, my signature move. I wonder what my career would have looked like had I not made the decision to change my style and add the back flip. Sure, I probably would have had a decent career, but it certainly wouldn't have had the pizzazz that it did with the back flip. It not only kept me feeling like I was evolving, but it brought to the audience something new and different.

Learn to Evolve with the Change

I like to say that there are three choices we have when faced with change: succumb, adapt, or evolve. *Succumbing* is giving up and not trying anymore. If the boss wants you to start using the Internet to reach clients but you decide you're too old to use a computer, you have given up and succumbed. If you learn the basic skills to appease your boss's wishes, then you have *adapted*. But if you take the challenge to change as an opportunity to grow and learn something new, you have made the best decision—now you can *evolve*. Evolving will make you more successful and ultimately happier with your life.

> If you take the challenge to change as an opportunity to grow and learn something new, you have made the best decision—now you can evolve.

Today, I am faced with this challenge. After taking more than four years off to focus on my health and my family, I have begun training again at a local rink. But I am much older, and a lot of things about my body have changed. I'm not as flexible, not as strong, not quite as fast. Yet I am also wiser. I will have to figure out if I know how to get the most out of the move and make it look better to an audience. But I am faced with the question: do I, or do I not, do the back flip? And will I do those signature triples that my fans have always come to be dazzled by?

My ego tells me, *Get out there and do it, old man! Show those young kids that you still got it.* But then my mind tells me that I am not the same skater, and I have to change, evolve my routine to better fit my physical capabilities.

I was talking on the phone the other day with my friend, Sam Miller, and he asked me, "Are you going to skate again?" I replied, "I don't know, Sam. Never say *never*."

Sam has known me a long time and has been around my skating for a long time. He asked me, "If you do, would you do those triple jumps and back flips?"

"Sam, I have to be honest with you," I said. "I don't know. Maybe."

Sam replies, "Look, let me tell you something, Scott. Don't tug on God's beard."

I thought that was wisdom beyond all wisdom. He was right. If I try to do something at fifty that I have no right to be doing beyond forty, then I am doing the equivalent of tugging on God's beard, that annoying little tug on Father Time's face.

If I skate again publicly, it will have to be different because I will be physically different. I learned this the hard way. Up until 2001, I clung to performing just as I always had, featuring the same moves and all the bells and whistles, maintaining a training regime that kept up the stamina and strength and skills needed to do that act. But looking back, for the next few years after that, rather than evolving, I did a mild, grade-B version of everything I had done. And then I stepped away for four years.

To come back now, I'd have to reinvent myself entirely because I'm not the same person physically, and I don't have the same kind of chronological momentum. It's like starting from scratch and presenting myself in a completely new and different way. I can't expect to be the performer that I was physically or artistically four years ago. It would be completely different. It would have to be. That's part of respecting God's plan.

Of course, I can let my ego interfere and try to do things I have no right to do. But then I wouldn't be happy. So many of us are unhappy because we are fighting against God's will, and we can never win that battle.

You can't fit into anyone else's mold but God's. I see a lot of unhappy people trying to fit into a mold that they desire or that our society pressures them into, but at the core it is not them; it is not natural.

If you're tugging on God's beard, He's going to have the last word every single time. I can accept the fact that I am older and come out with a watered-down act. I can try to do a cheaper version of my old routine with half versions of everything I used to do. Or I can evolve and come up with a brand-new routine, with new moves that aren't as technically challenging but can still wow a crowd. Evolving in response to the change is always the best option. If it's the fall, you can't walk around dressed for summer in shorts and a T-shirt. The season of my life has changed, and I have to change with it. You, too, have to learn a new routine and embrace the season you are in right now.

MAKING THE RIGHT DECISIONS

When it comes to relationships, whether personal or professional, evolving and making the right decisions for change can be especially challenging. I saw this dilemma play out in a public way with Kristi Yamaguchi and Rudy Galindo. They were a National Champion pairs team in 1989 and 1990 and made it to the top five at the World Championships several years in a row. They did perfect side-by-side jumps and overall were pretty good, but not as good as the Russians and a lot of the other teams out there.

By 1990, Kristi had a budding singles career and was moving up that ladder. It got to a point where Kristi, who was nineteen years old, had to figure out what was in the best interest of her skating career. She clearly could no longer do pairs and singles at the same time and be world-class at both. If she did, she would never be 100 percent of anything. But up until then, Kristi was best known as Rudy's partner, and Rudy had hoped they could compete together and win gold at the 1992 Olympics. Kristi had to make a choice, and she chose to end her pairs career to focus exclusively on her singles career.

> When it comes to relationships, whether personal or professional, evolving and making the right decisions for change can be especially challenging.

Rudy was devastated and couldn't believe that she had done this to him. Kristi felt terrible about how he reacted and, because she is a sensitive person, didn't like that she had hurt him. He actually wrote about it in his autobiography, how he felt betrayed and deserted by her. Rudy was very bitter about it, although there was no question in anyone else's mind that Kristi, who was good in pairs but had potential to be great in singles, had made the right decision. This proved to be the case when she won the World Figure Skating Championships in 1991 and 1992 and the Gold Medal at the 1992 Olympics.

Kristi evolved, though it meant making a very hard decision to break it off with Rudy. I would hear Rudy talk about the heartache he felt when his pairs career ended with Kristi. But I thought he was missing the big picture. He went on to have a phenomenal singles career himself, winning the US men's title in 1996 and bronze in the Worlds that same year. He then had a very long and successful pro touring career as a solo skater. None of the greatest accomplishments of his life could have happened had he stayed in the pair with Kristi. But it happened almost in spite of himself because for so many years, he resisted that change. All of us have probably been Rudy Galindo or Kristi Yamaguchi at some time in our life. We have broken hearts, have walked away from something that hurt someone else, or had someone leave us, but in the end the change was for the better and we were happier for it.

> It's a fact of life that your definition of happiness will change as you change.

It's a fact of life that your definition of happiness will change as you change. My definition of happiness has changed as I have progressed through life. Early in my career, happiness meant winning the Gold Medal. Then it meant making as much money as possible as a pro. Finally, true happiness came to mean not only being a great athlete and artist but also being a well-rounded human being and enjoying my family.

Your definition of happiness will also change with time, but to find any kind of happiness you need to start with knowing exactly what you're seeking, see it happening, repeat the steps it takes to get there—and then be willing to change course as things change. That's the mark of every champion of happiness.

CHAPTER EIGHT

STAND IN THE SPOTLIGHT

Assuming you've read this book chronologically, you've already learned nearly everything you need to know about how to be happy. The only thing left is to apply these principles to your daily life with the focus, discipline, and dedication of a championship figure skater.

You are the secret to finding happiness. *You* hold the keys to unlocking the door to a happier life. It's time for you to step into the spotlight.

Consider yourself an athlete competing in a sport called happiness. The goal is to win the game, and to do so you need to have a strategy. That's exactly what I've already outlined for you in this book:

- Fall, Get Up, and Land Your First Jumps
- Trust Your Almighty Coach
- Make Your Losses Your Wins
- Keep the Ice Clear
- Think Positive, Laugh, and Smile Like Kristi Yamaguchi
- Win by Going Last
- Learn a New Routine

The eighth and final secret is for you to stand in the spotlight and to skate your best, to incorporate all you've learned and to do the work it takes to look at life like an optimist.

> During the few months it took me to write this book, I had to practice every secret that I have shared.

The hard fact is that you don't become a happy person overnight, just as one doesn't instantly become a world-class skater. Much like a skater hones his technique, you have to practice the fundamentals of finding happiness every day. And, yes, I am not immune to the obstacles. I am just like anyone else in that happiness sometimes can be a daily struggle.

In fact, even during the few months it took me to write this book, I had to practice every secret that I have shared.

FACING ANOTHER SETBACK

Oddly enough, I started feeling a sense of discontentment and unhappiness after I began the process of making a skating comeback (my second one since my cancer battle). I had started skating and training in the hopes of being able to perform in front of a live audience again. Whenever I had taken breaks from skating in the past, support—from fans, the media, the skating community at large—was always there, typically with great fanfare. I had not skated professionally in more than four years, ever since my brain tumor diagnosis, but I had been thinking seriously about returning to the ice.

It seemed like the perfect time. The idea of coming back in my fiftieth year on the planet, while also celebrating the twenty-fifth anniversary of my Olympic Gold Medal win, seemed like the kind of perfect storm of forces that would excite everyone. I was sure there would be a lot of support for my "big comeback" after being away for four-plus years.

One of the first people I told about my comeback was a friend in Nashville who is a very successful singer-songwriter. He had tried to talk me into coming out of retirement more than a year earlier, but I had a lot of excuses why I wasn't ready: I had a baby, I was too old, I was too sick, I had nothing left to prove. But after a lot of thought and prayer, I realized those weren't reasons not to skate—rather, they were excuses for not doing what I knew in my heart I so desperately wanted, and possibly needed, to feel like I was living a truly fulfilling life.

Spiritually, I had known for some time I had to make a comeback. Soon after Aidan was born, skating began to dominate my thoughts. One Sunday as I drove to church, I asked God to give me a sign as to what I should do. I was debating whether to hang up the skates for good, and I simply couldn't figure it out.

I got to church, sat down, and a fellow congregant began the service with a reading of Psalm 121:3: "He will not let your foot slip" (NIV). That line hit me like a bucket of water in the face. I knew right then exactly what God's plan was for me, that eventually I would come back, that it was my calling. It was just a matter of when.

As expected, my friend was confident that I was going to inspire many people with a return to the ice, not to mention believing that I would become a happier person in the process.

One potential part of the plan was to produce a television special, or possibly a series, documenting my comeback. So in early 2008, I went to LA and met with some of the top television producers in the business, some of whom I considered friends, and shared my idea. They said all the right things. Almost across the board, everyone reacted with excitement. It seemed like the TV piece of the puzzle was practically a shoo-in.

Then they stopped returning my calls.

I don't know why. I can only draw my own conclusions. Amid my disappointment that the TV world wasn't moving with the speed and enthusiasm I had hoped for, another setback happened. I pulled my right groin muscle doing a simple double lutz while working out with my longtime choreographer, Sarah Kawahara. It was the third time I had pulled this muscle in the process of making my comeback. The first time was on a Saturday morning session at my home rink in Nashville. I didn't want to miss many days of practice, so I went to the rink on what would normally be a day off. I was working through the jumps and got up to the double lutz. It had been going well in the previous workouts, and I wanted to keep up the repetitions.

The session was crowded, and it took me a few times around the rink to fit one in. It was then that I felt the tug on the groin muscle that would soon be something more than I wanted to deal with. I left the lutz alone for a few days and tried it again later the next week. It pulled again. And in a way that I should have realized that leaving the jump out of my workouts should have been my first decision. But I wanted to show off everything to Sarah. We had worked together for more than twenty years, and she was surprised at the level I had achieved in so little time.

But this pull was not good. I knew immediately that it was a severe pull with tearing that wouldn't heal quickly. In fact, it could require at least a couple of months of rehab. Injury was a fear I had from the very beginning. I was pushing fifty, after all. Injuries would pose the greatest threat to my return. And just a few months into my comeback, I suffered one of the worst injuries a skater can get. But I wasn't about to let it stop me altogether. I mean, in my prime I skated with worse injuries. I didn't want to let a groin yank scare me into submission.

> Just a few months into my comeback, I suffered one of the worst injuries a skater can get.

Sarah had helped me make a comeback from my cancer in 1998. Like the last time, she had given me a lot of drills and foot-work, coordinating moves to get my body and strength and flexibility back. She said, "I don't know what to expect, but I am optimistic." She liked what she was seeing. I thought I would get stronger and my jumps bigger. My spins were starting to happen, and my feet got lighter and faster. And then came the pull. That injury put me way back. Of all things to go wrong, that was the last thing I wanted to happen. I just needed to get to that healthy place again. I was almost there. I began to doubt whether I could come back, and the thought of not being able to sent me into a horrible funk.

The pulled groin, coupled with the lack of movement on the TV front, broke my spirit. I started feeling sorry for myself. Poor Scott. Yet another setback. If it's not a life-threatening illness, it's an injury of some sort. Poor, poor, old me.

And so I just stopped skating completely. That's right. Mr. Optimism, Mr. Think Positive, Mr. How-to-Be-Happy himself simply gave up.

Soon after, I was talking to my Nashville friend, and he asked how my skating was going. I told him of my disappointments, and he shared something with me. He had been secretly doing a lot of writing. Not just songs but a book. He was writing every day, dedicating himself to the process and feeling pretty good about it.

He had recently sent it to a friend who was very well respected in the literary world. He is a very successful songwriter, but since book writing was new to him, he was understandably insecure about how it would be received and if a publisher would be interested.

His friend read the first two-hundred-fifty pages, but she didn't give him the feedback he was looking for. Instead, she said, "I could edit it down to fifty really good ones."

He was hurt by her feedback, stunned that something that he had poured his heart and soul into was, according to at least one respected reader, not up to snuff. It really upset him. She probably meant it as a compliment, but it broke his heart.

But then he thought about it more and came to realize that he likes the *process* of writing. He likes what he is writing. It makes him happy. Why should he let someone take that away from him because she might be looking at it from a different point of view? He decided that he would take her criticism under advisement, but he would keep writing because he enjoyed it. If someone else wants to read it or publish it, then fine. If not, that's okay too. He is plowing forward, and he told me I should do the same.

There was a great lesson in what he was saying. Actually, I had been writing about that very lesson in my own book! Make your losses your wins, think positive, learn a new routine—nearly everything I had been writing about could be applied to my own situation.

I had to accept the fact that not everything would work out precisely the way I wanted it to, and I had to take a deeper look at why I was returning to skating. Regaining my physical and mental health was first and foremost. Ever since I was a kid, I was physically healthier when I was skating. Ice always helped me feel better throughout my life. I am healthiest when I am on the ice, have a schedule, and have a level of fitness. Without it, I feel like I am struggling a bit. And I was pretty good, even when I was skating with an undiagnosed brain tumor.

So why did I totally abandon skating? The more I examined my departure, the more I concluded that I had retired (unofficially) because I feared I couldn't live up to others' expectations. I had given everyone else the power to make me happy as a skater. Once

I accepted that the act of returning to the ice itself was a big enough pot of gold for me, I was able to refocus. I got back on the ice and, as of now, I am skating and improving enough to make me happy. And that is what matters most.

I had thought it was all or nothing, but like most everything in life, it is about finding a balance.

KNOW HOW TO GET UP

As I mentioned earlier, one of the first things they teach kids learning how to skate is how to get up after falling down. It is a challenge to get upright on your blades when you are having trouble just standing up, but since it is certain that all beginners will fall, they first have to know how to get up! What a great life lesson. We will all fail; we will all suffer the metaphorical equivalent of landing a lutz with a jolt of pain. It is inevitable. But it is accepting this fact and knowing how to pull yourself up that gets you back on the road to happiness.

> I had thought it was all or nothing, but like most everything in life, it is about finding a balance.

Skating is a great school for life, a great teacher of how to achieve a goal one step at a time and how to use perseverance and patience along the way. You first learn how to skate forward, one stride at a time. Then comes skating backward. And when you get those basics down, you're ready to learn how to do crossovers, placing one leg over the other to change directions. Being able to skate in every direction, you then can work on improving your balance through working on inside and outside edge movements along the figure eight.

Only then, after what can be a year or two of practice, are you even ready to begin learning the fun stuff—the basic jumps and spins of freestyle figure skating: salchows, toe loops, loops, flips, lutzes, axels. Each movement is learned only after you've perfected the one before it. But once you learn how to do each correctly, they will be yours for life.

> I have provided a map, but it's up to you to get yourself to the destination of happiness.

The same can be said of the fundamentals of finding happiness in your life. It takes a discipline of focus and determination to achieve happiness. And no one will make it happen for you but yourself. I have provided a map, but it's up to you to get yourself to the destination of happiness.

It takes a lot of hard work. But if it were easy to achieve, then everyone would be happy. A very good comparison to what it takes to be happy is what it took me to build up to being a world-class skater.

COMMIT TO THE PROCESS

As I mentioned earlier, when I began skating as a kid, I would see older skaters doing amazing tricks and acrobatic moves, and I wanted to be that good right away. I was a very impatient little boy, and it frustrated me that I couldn't just go out there and land lutzes and toe loops and spin like a top. I wanted to be free to do all these amazingly athletic things with my body and bring a crowd to their feet and win.

But then, as coaches showed me what it would take for me to get to that place, I realized that about a third of my total score would come from how well I did the compulsory figures competition. That meant that what I would be judged by would have nothing to do with spinning, jumping, leaping, or anything remotely fun to a nine-year-old boy. Rather, I would have to learn how to trace single circular lines into the ice on one foot, over and over and over again until I was able to trace over them to perfection. The reason for the compulsory tests is to separate the showboats from the technically sound skaters. But while I didn't care to be technically sound, coaches taught me that I would never be the champion I aspired to become without developing the strength, balance, and focus that comes with mastering the fundamentals. Since I wanted to win as much as I wanted to entertain, I decided to commit to the process.

In order to excel at the compulsory figures, you must use so many little muscles and all of your athletic wherewithal to execute them. It's almost mind-boggling to think about balancing on a quarter-inch width of steel, traveling at a slow walking speed and having to draw a perfect arc, and then tracing it within a quarter-inch precision in order to be on a competitive level. But skaters get to that place by showing up every day, committing themselves to the process, and applying all the fundamental skills necessary. So it is with finding happiness and fulfillment in your life. You need to commit to the process, no matter how laborious or tedious or tough.

There are a lot of quick schemes out there. Get rich quick. Get thin quick. Get out of debt quick. You name it, and it seems someone is trying to sell us on the idea that we can get things done quickly. But in my experience, anything truly worth having takes commitment to it over a long period of time before you can get it. Let's say that you could get perfect abs overnight. So then what? I mean, how satisfying would it be if you could get them that fast? Anything that you can achieve in a short period of time will only be realized by taking shortcuts that end up backfiring on you. Just ask all the guys out there who used steroids to get ripped muscles only to suffer from muscle tears, heart problems, and shrinking testicles. A shortcut, indeed, is the longest distance between two points.

So it is with finding happiness and fulfillment in your life. You need to commit to the process, no matter how laborious or tedious or tough.

Those who have successfully battled their weight will tell you that they didn't find long-term success at dropping—and keeping off—the weight until they committed to a long-term program. You can pop a pill that will burn some fat. You can follow some goofy, expensive supplement diet that requires you to drink green shakes seven times a day. But then reality kicks in and the idea of you drinking those shakes or popping pills for the rest of your life is just not realistic. You have to restrict your calories, exercise daily, and eat a balanced diet. But chances are that you're not going to totally transition to this new lifestyle overnight. At first, you will miss those double bacon cheeseburgers and Hostess cupcakes because you've built up certain tastes and habits over such a long period of time. You will get off track and break your diet. But if you break it down to being committed every day, over time, you will see amazing changes in how you look and feel.

Similarly, there is no get-happy-quick scheme that can guarantee you lasting happiness and fulfillment overnight. But if you commit to the process of the great eight secrets of happiness, making the right choices day after day, you will begin to experience the happiness for which you've been looking.

Only You Can Let the Light Inside

Our pop culture gets a lot of deserved criticism for its more vapid representations. But for every celebrity meltdown or mind-numbing sitcom, there is the occasional gem of inspiration. I know that fifty-year-old men aren't exactly the demographic for MTV, but I am a fan of the theme song of the network's reality show *The Hills*. The tune, sung by the British singer Natasha Bedingfield, is called "Unwritten," and my favorite line is one that is very fitting to the theme of this book: "Today is where your book begins."

I can offer advice, share my stories of how I learned how to be happy (even when I had every reason to be miserable). But when it comes down to it, only you can live the happy life that God wants you to live and fill the pages of your life's unwritten book. Only you can step into the spotlight of your life.

I recently told someone I was writing this book. "What's it about?"

my friend asked. I replied, "I guess it's kind of a guide to optimism. It's about how to be happy."

She flashed the biggest smile and said, "I love that! I want to read that." And with all humility, who wouldn't? I mean, we all want to be happy, even though we all might do things that keep us from being happy. But while we all want to reach that destination, not all of us are willing to do what it takes to get there. This book is a guide, but once you put down this book, you have an entire life to lead in which you must practice what I have preached.

Commitment. Repetition. These are words that scare a lot of people today. These kinds of words drive people away from diets and workout plans and even marriages. So many of us want things to be *fun* or *dynamic* or an *adventure*. If people think there's no fun in it and that they will have to deprive themselves or change something they don't want to change, they will avoid doing it. But I'm telling you that if you want to be happy

> If you commit to the process of the great eight secrets of happiness, making the right choices day after day, you will begin to experience the happiness for which you've been looking.

with anything in your life, if you want to have more fun with your life, it isn't something you can go buy at a discount store for a few dollars and suddenly possess. Yet it's not as difficult as it may seem if you see your life as what it already is: perfect.

I'm looking at my little boy Maxx right now. He's rolling around on the floor, barely able to crawl, just a perfect little creature. He's going to face challenges. He's going to have issues. He's going to have anxieties and fears and disappointments, and people are going to hurt him physically and mentally and emotionally. That's life, and I can't protect him from all that stuff entirely, but I can give him this net to fall into: "You are perfect." I firmly believe God made us in His image, and that is a perfect one. Tracie and I tell Aidan that regardless of how people treat him or what they say or do, whether they're young or old or thin or big or whatever color they are, they're positively perfect in God's eyes. We're no better than they, and they're no better than us. We're all perfect. And it's such a healthy way to live each day.

FIND YOUR FOURTH ANGEL

One of the biggest barriers to people feeling happy about themselves is that they feel inferior, or shameful and bad about their looks or something in their past. But once you see yourself as a truly perfect creature created in God's image who only needs to get in touch with that, the pressure of all those negative feelings lifts and you can move on. It is life changing.

Everyone needs a helping hand. When I was going through my cancer battle, I couldn't have done it without the help of others. I called them my cancer angels. My oncologist was my first angel. He was the one who was treating me and giving me what I needed in order to get my physical health back. My second angel was my oncology nurse. She was there at the front line, administering all the stuff that the oncologist wanted done. My third angel revelaed itself through my friends and family. They were there to support me emotionally.

But you always need that fourth angel. The fourth angel is someone who's been there, done that, someone who can give you the life coaching you need. It's not about giving medical advice; it's about saying, "I've been where you are. I was diagnosed with the same illness, I've had the same treatments, and I'm here alive to tell you about it. Here's how I handled it. And here's how I wish I would have handled this." Your fourth angel isn't someone who is going to feel sorry for you—he knows where you're coming from. On those horrible days when you're feeling at your lowest, your fourth angel is somebody on the other end of the phone or sitting across the table from you who has lived everything that you're going through right now and is a great role model, a great coach, a great person to lean on for support.

> The fourth angel is someone who's been there, done that, someone who can give you the life coaching you need.

In so many ways, that fourth angel is what I'm trying to be for you with this book. I have felt that pain. I have felt that anxiety. I have felt that loss. I have felt that fear. I have felt that disappointment. I have been hurt. I have been chewed up and spat out. And I have been betrayed. The chapters in this book tell you how I have managed not only to deal with it but also to conquer it.

I was lucky to have many fourth angels throughout my life, including my parents, coaches, sponsors, business associates, people in the media, doctors, and cancer survivors. That's why I started The 4th Angel Mentoring Program, which is a centerpiece of my Cancer Alliance for Research, Education, and Survivorship (CARES) initiative at the Cleveland Clinic's Taussig Cancer Center. I started the program, after surviving my battle, to encourage cancer survivors to help other cancer patients as mentors. They provide comfort, reassurance, information, coping techniques, and practical advice.

I have discovered that one of the keys to finding happiness is to look around and find people to whom you can be a *fourth angel*. Whether you are currently experiencing a difficult situation or looking back on something you've survived, there are many ways you can reach out to help others who are going through a similar situation. I encourage you to ask people in your local church and community center or even to search online for ways you can mentor others through their tough times and be a fourth angel to them.

More than anything, I hope that this book will serve as your fourth angel and that the great eight secrets of happiness I have shared will help you be happy and experience the life God intended for you to enjoy.

Acknowledgments

In appreciation to the countless people who made each moment happen, whether or not they ever realized their contributions to the quality of my life, I give special thanks to:

Ken Baker for convincing me to make this book happen.

Larry Thompson, my friend, mentor, and manager, for believing in me. Your wisdom and points of view have taken me to another level, personally and professionally.

Bob Kain for making such an amazing impact on my life.

Kristi Yamaguchi, Steven Cousins, Kurt Browning, Paul Wylie, Rosalyn Sumners, Katarina Witt, Katia Gordeeva, Brian Orser, Ilia Kulik, Joe Sabovcik, Denis Petrov, Jayne Torvill, Peter and Kitty

Carruthers, and my parallel life friend, Chistopher Dean, for all the incredible moments on and off the ice.

Kevin, Susan, and Gable Nealon; Brad, Kim, and Huck Paisley; Bill and Liz Shatner; David and Cathy Michaels; Eric and Tanya Idle; and Ken and Nancy Durham for friendship, laughter, and unconditional love and support.

Sam and Maria Miller. You have made a profound impact on the world and on me and my family. Together we will keep pushing to find a cure for cancer.

Sterling and Stacy Ball. Thanks for "adopting" me. Being in your family has been a blast!

Jane Dystel and Miriam Goderich for being so instrumental in this project.

Debbie Wickwire and everyone at Thomas Nelson Publishers for making the process of preparing this book so enjoyable.

And most important: my sons, Aidan and Maxx. Every day you make me want to be a better person. I hope this book will make you proud of me.

ABOUT THE AUTHOR

Scott Hamilton, the most popular and beloved male figure-skating star in the world, is also a network-TV skating commentator, an actor, performer, producer, Emmy Award nominee, best-selling author, role model, humanitarian, philanthropist, and cancer and brain tumor survivor.

Scott is constantly reminding others that with fortitude and determination, anything is possible. He has become a much sought-after motivational speaker, speaking about his life and overcoming cancer, for a wide variety of groups and organizations from as small as five hundred to as large as fifteen thousand.

Scott appears regularly on television and is a popular guest on national news shows, such as the *Today Show*; and entertainment news programs, such as *Access Hollywood*, *Inside Edition*, *The Insider*, *Extra!*, *E! Entertainment*, the *TV Guide Channel*, and *Entertainment Tonight*; and in various national news publications, such as *People* magazine. He made his motion picture debut in *On Edge*, a hilarious 2001 mockumentary of figure skating, and starred in the recent, mega box-office hit, motion picture comedy *Blades of Glory*, with Will Ferrell and Jon Heder.

As an author, Scott received notable critical praise for his *New York Times* best-selling autobiography *Landing It* (Kensington Books, October 1999), an intimate, candid, and insightful look at his professional and personal life on and off the ice.

Audiences have watched Scott perform with numerous US symphony orchestras, in his own *Scott Hamilton's America Tour*, and in fifteen national touring seasons with Stars on Ice, which he also cocreated and served as coproducer until his retirement from the tour in April 2001. For two seasons since then, he returned to Stars on Ice as a special guest star in select cities, and he continues to be the creative producing force behind each annual production.

During a fourteen-year tenure with the CBS Television Network as one of its most articulate sports analysts, Scott covered multiple Olympic Games. He recently signed a three-year exclusive agreement with NBC Sports to cover all of the network's skating broadcasts, including the Winter Olympics in 2010.

To add to a remarkable list of achievements, which now includes over seventy titles, awards, and honors, Scott was inducted in 1990 into the United States Olympic Hall of Fame. In that same year, he also became a privileged member of the World Figure Skating Hall of Fame.

On December 14, 2002, at a small, very private ceremony held in Malibu, California, Scott married former nutritionist, Tracie Robinson. It was the first marriage for both. On September 16, 2003, Tracie gave birth to the couple's first child, Aidan McIntosh Hamilton. Their second child, Maxx Thomas Hamilton, was born January 21, 2008.

When he is not working or performing or participating in a wide variety of charitable events, acting as an official spokesperson for Target House at St. Jude Children's Hospital in Memphis, Tennessee, as well as his own Scott Hamilton CARES Initiative (Cancer Alliance for Research, Education, and Survivorship) at the Cleveland Clinic Taussig Center in Cleveland, Ohio, or promoting his Web site, www.Chemocare.com (in conjunction with the Cleveland Clinic and CARES), or serving on the Board of Directors for Special Olympics, Scott can be found on the golf course and enjoys spending time with his wife and two sons at their home in Nashville, Tennessee.

KEN BAKER, a brain tumor survivor, is a pop culture journalist and executive news editor for *E!*. He's also the author of three books, including two memoirs: *Man Made* and *They Don't Play Hockey in Heaven*.